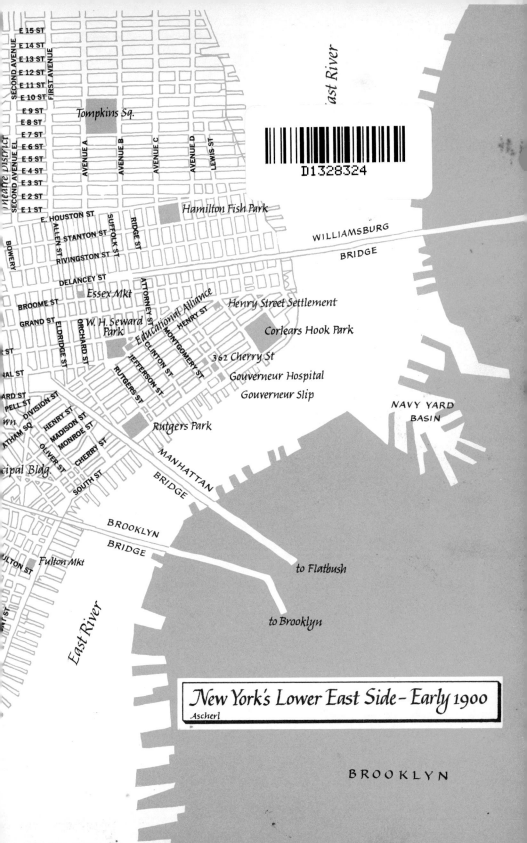

New York's Lower East Side - Early 1900

Ascherl

East River

WILLIAMSBURG BRIDGE

E 15 ST
E 14 ST
E 13 ST
E 12 ST
E 11 ST
E 10 ST
E 9 ST
E 8 ST
E 7 ST
E 6 ST
E 5 ST
E 4 ST
E 3 ST
E 2 ST
E 1 ST

SECOND AVENUE
FIRST AVENUE
AVENUE A
AVENUE B
AVENUE C
AVENUE D
LEWIS ST

Theatre District
SECOND AVENUE EL

Tompkins Sq.

Hamilton Fish Park

E. HOUSTON ST
ALLEN ST
STANTON ST
RIVINGSTON ST
SUFFOLK ST
RIDGE ST

BOWERY

DELANCEY ST

Essex Mkt

BROOME ST
GRAND ST

W. H. Seward Park

Educational Alliance

ATTORNEY ST
HENRY ST
MONTGOMERY ST
CLINTON ST

Henry Street Settlement

Corlears Hook Park

362 Cherry St

Gouverneur Hospital

Gouverneur Slip

NAVY YARD BASIN

ORCHARD ST
ELDRIDGE ST

JEFFERSON ST
RUTGERS ST

NAL ST

ARD ST
PELL ST

wn
DIVISION ST

ATHAM SQ

HENRY ST
MADISON ST
MONROE ST

Rutgers Park

OLIVER ST
CHERRY ST

cipal Bldg

SOUTH ST

MANHATTAN BRIDGE

BROOKLYN BRIDGE

to Flatbush

to Brooklyn

FULTON ST

Fulton Mkt

East River

RST

BROOKLYN

rnors Is.

THE TIME THAT WAS THEN

Also by Harry Roskolenko

Novels:

Black Is A Man
Lan-Lan

Autobiography:

When I Was Last On Cherry Street
The Terrorized
The Time That Was Then

Poetry:

Sequence on Violence
I Went Into The Country
A Second Summary, illustrated by Sidney Nolan
Notes from a Journey, illustrated by Sidney Nolan
Paris Poems, illustrated by Zao Wou-Ki
American Civilization, illustrated by John Olsen, Clifton Pugh, Albert Tucker

Travel:

Poet on a Scooter
White Man, Go!

THE TIME
THAT WAS THEN

The Lower East Side
1900–1914
An Intimate Chronicle

by

Harry Roskolenko

The Dial Press *New York, 1971*

To my sisters and brothers:
Edna, Herschel, Mike, Bill . . .
and to Patricia Edwards Clyne

Contents

THE TIME THAT WAS THEN

Chapter 1

Prologue: Once Upon An Immigrant . . .

It was another time and another place, then, on Cherry Street. It was the lowest part of the East Side amid crowded-together, five-story, wash-hung tenements. Everything was immigrant laden, a bazaar of colors and bizarre languages. It was 1907 and a year of panic.

I was born into a self-contained Yiddish ghetto. Though we were the majority, the ghetto also housed Poles, Russians, Irish, and Italians. All of us had our special places, dictated to us by our faces, our speech, our jobs, our music, dances, and books—and, of course, our religion and country of origin. Each one lived in a ghetto within a ghetto. Did we mind it? We wanted to be among our own people, our own language, our own religion, and to be ourselves down to our last Jewish roots.

Home came equipped with a fire escape for summer sleeping—an iron porch open to the world. Every floor had four railroad flats. On our floor, the one toilet in the hall served the four families—two Jewish, one Russian, and one Polish. There was a yard in back and a house in the rear, two stories high. Here, in their own selectivity, lived the poorer of the poor—in back, unable to see what went on in the tumbling, fierce activity and continuous gabble of the strident streets.

HARRY ROSKOLENKO

The architecture was created some time before 1870 by the Tenement Houses Building Company, by variously borrowed English conceptions for mass housing for the poor—and by the Tenement House Law enacted in 1901 to safeguard the poverty of the poor from the hazards of the planners, the builders, and the city's early breed of real-estate profiteers.

But whether you lived in the front house or in the rear house, it was a home if your parents made it a home. We had a Russian-Jewish home that included three beds in tiers, warmed by a Russian stove; a samovar; huge, downy comforters; great, soft pillows; Jewish charity boxes; no pictures; mirrors that faced the wall—to offset vanity, my mother said, though this was traditionally done for mourning. The stove, a mammoth iron and brick affair, had been built by my father and took care of all heating and cooking needs. We had towel racks, boxes and bottles for cereals, tea, and vegetables, ice in the icebox—and six children warmed by my two God-graced parents.

We wore what my father could buy for us. It meant old clothes, bought secondhand, for school and for play, and new clothes, firsthand for the Sabbath. My father, skilled and un-skilled, had no trade worth much when I was a child. He was, at times, a cloak presser, which paid little in wages and took its sad toll of his health. I used to see him sweating in a Greene Street factory during the summer, steam rising from the heavy pressing iron and enshrouding his thin body. Scars across his naked back recalled the lashes of the tsarist *nagaika* from his soldiering days. Another trade, earlier, had taken him to the slaughterhouse of Wilson & Company on First Avenue, on the site where the UN keeps the peace of the world today.

Before coming to America he had been a Jewish peasant in the Ukraine. He had run a mill, as well. A man of the land, he was to spend most of his life in sweatshops after he arrived, in 1895, at the age of thirty-five. And he was never to know anything good no matter where he worked in New York. For it was the wrong time for a man of half skills who preferred God to the making of money to be in the United States of America.

12

My mother, who was not financially illiterate, was soon calling America "America *Gonef*" (America the thief).

My father, named Barnett, was called Berel by all—and no one understood how he had gotten that English name. He was five feet five inches tall, slender, brown-eyed, half bald, whimsical, hardly a great scholar, but sufficiently learned in the endless concerns of Judaism. His small black-gray beard, which he trimmed for the Sabbath, made him look like a doctor who had too many patients without money. To see him walking in the street, most professorial and dignified, was hardly to recall that he was a cloak presser, a leader of a Judas goat, a man with half skills who looked too neat for the slaughtering century that had just begun.

My mother, Chai-Sura (Sarah), lived for God's graces even more than my father did. Short, a peasant by her way of talking and walking, she was blond, blue-eyed, and high-cheeked. She had a rosy glow and God figured endlessly in her conversation. She could neither read nor write, but she memorized every prayer and ritual, and knew as much as the old rabbi did at the *shul* on Madison Street off Montgomery.

God was in every mystery for my mother. *Gehenna* (hell) was there as well. And *Gan Eden* (heaven) would assuredly come the "day after the day after." Gan Eden was a mystery she was always trying to unravel for me, and when I told her that Catholics and Muslims also believed in the hereafter, I would get a small lecture about the impossibility of God's existing for anybody but us—the chosen of the chosen. When I said that there were Negro Jews in Harlem, she was astonished at first and later insisted that I had invented them. When I was ten years old and I asked her, "What if your daughter Edna wanted to marry a Negro Jew—what would you do?" she slapped my face and that ended my sociological explorations. For my mother there was only God, Gehenna and Gan Eden—the hereafter for all good Jews on Cherry Street.

Cherry Street had great traditions, we knew. It had once been most important. Even George Washington had had his

13

official home there in the early days of the republic. As kids we reenacted this bit of history and selected sides. One side became the British redcoats, the other the Colonials, and the leader took over as George Washington himself. We battled by land and by sea. It was our way of acting out American history in fact and in legend—as new Americans.

Three blocks south of Cherry Street ran the East River to the Lower Bay and out to the Atlantic Ocean, with ships going to every port in the world. It was later to become the liquid route that I took to leave the ghetto's circumscribed interior life, the squat-smelly streets—and my parents' Judaism. The East River was my Jordan River, crossing into the unknown Gentile world of other woes, fears, and disguises.

I had almost drowned in that river when I went sailing to the Statue of Liberty on a raft. The river was my refuge when I needed to escape from fatherly rebukes, minor beatings, garbaged streets, dead horses, shrill laments—and the rabbi. Then I would sit on a decaying pier under the Manhattan Bridge or the Brooklyn Bridge and watch freighters slide through the scummy river; or old schooners that still had golden figureheads under the foresail; or the hustling ferries going to Brooklyn, passing the fishing boats that put in at Fulton Street with a load of fish just caught in the Atlantic. The piers were my second home—before and after the synagogue's spiritual ravishment.

I was part of a once-large family, but only six of us were left —four boys and two girls, all born on the Lower East Side. In the Ukraine, before the turn of the industrializing and ravaging century, eight others had been borne by my stolid mother. They had died in infancy in those times of easy dying. But we, Americans all, were tougher, burlier, hardier, and better fed. We were another set of health statistics. We had more possibilities, if less of God; though my father tried to give us both with the bread my mother baked, the wine he made, and the guided spiritualism of a man who was as Old Testament as Moses with his stern, fatherly hand.

14

THE TIME THAT WAS THEN

The vast migrations from Eastern Europe created the Jewish ghettos on the Lower East Side. What cities and villages did the new arrivals not come from? The place-names, like the burial societies and other *vereins*, have their own sociological myths today. When you talked Yiddish, you did it with a special accent, as you did English. We were either Litvaks or Galicians, and soon somebody was laughing at the heavy accents with which we pronounced words like *bread* and *butter*. But we laughed loudest at the Hungarian Jews, for they had the funniest and broadest accents on the block. And, occasionally, the teasing about accents would start a fistfight. Over bread? Over butter? It was insane in a happy Jewish kind of way.

But whoever our neighbors were and no matter from where they came, they had, like my parents, come with bundles, bags, old books, downy pillows, feather comforters in red-pink coverings, copper pots, samovars, candlesticks for the Sabbath, and menorahs for lighting up a golden holiday.

All of them were seeking the *Goldeneh Medina*—the Golden Land—within a few square miles of the Lower East Side. But what they found became New York's triumphs and tragedies of reckless architecture, sudden slums, terrible factories—and the high-rises that still signify rush, hurry, ghetto gutting, and today's city living and dying from every pore. They had come in a hurry in the holds of ships, to build the *Medina* in the New World. They had come from something much worse, but between 1900 and 1970 they and their sons contributed much of what we have today, including the garment industry, the jewelry trades, the retail shops, the current medical and dental professions, and some of New York's searing landscape.

It was a long haul for all. It was a time for speed, not for permanent values. It was the time for mass living, mass production, mass consumption—and the massing city was unable to plan for anything but immediate living space.

The Jewish immigrants, from my parents' total view, had enough sustenance in their vision of God; though God was hardly enough in tough New York's mammoth encampment. But

15

if God was enough for men like my father, their sons, in time, changed the tokens of value. God became success. Success became money. The rigid rituals and values of Judaism were changed by default. Their sons, of course, joined the temples of worship. But going there on the High Holy Days did not make them *frume Yidn*—religious Jews. In my time we had called the temples *shuls*. They were simple buildings, primitive, hardly worth an architect's time. We went there to pray, not to play bingo and run raffles. We had one purpose—to go to God. All our words were God-graced and we were humble as we prayed and sang about the glories of the Lord on Cherry Street.

That has changed, of course. America, as an image, has changed the edifice, the manner, if not all the tokens of faith. The American way, for all of us, from Jews to Gentiles, has given us the vulgar interludes of added attractions to a fading faith. The dollar's green sign hangs seen and unseen from churches and synagogues. Faith is not enough today. The dollar and doubt are more inspirational, at times. The "Big Giver" and the sociological lecturer have replaced the moral and spiritual leader who guided my father in his time.

When I was a child, New York was the natural Mecca for the immigrants coming to the New World. And every letter to my father, written in Russian, Polish, or Hebrew, from some relative in our Ukrainian village, Zareby Koscielne, usually ended with the question. "When will you send money for a *shifskart*?"

The ship's ticket was a passport to Cherry Street, East Broadway, Delancey Street, night school—to all of the United States taking in the huddled masses. It was a ticket to family honor— redeemed at Ellis Island by brothers, sisters, cousins, uncles, and friends. It was money given like a grant-in-aid, rather than as a returnable loan. It was blood money in its most honorable sense—money given so that others of one's clan could get to Ellis Island, and, soon enough, to the Orchard Streets all over the hustling, emerging United States of America.

When the newest arrival was picked up at the huge immigration terminus, he or she was soon bedded down in my father's house. Cots were pulled out. Children's sleeping arrangements were doubled up. The kitchen became a bedroom. The living room was a room for everything, especially for mass meetings of relatives.

How was everybody in Zareby Koscielne? Who was the rabbi? Had the *shul* gone under? Was Uncle David still on his farm? How many cows did he have? What, a new wife? His fifth? Such strength! How many children does he have now? An army full!

"God should forbid such things," said my mother.

"Why?" asked my father. "Uncle David is built like a bull—and what should a bull do?"

Within a month the new arrivals had jobs, a flat, and they were saving money for other members of the Roskolenko tribe left over in Zareby Koscielne. And that was the way a minor portion of a street in New York City was settled, the unions built, the sweatshops worked in, new trades learned, new children born, new *shuls* attended. The studious traveled even farther. Those who could afford to study and manage to work their way into the professions left the pushcarts and the sweatshops to their fathers—for American-made professional bargains. For all of us soon learned that the green dollar did not grow on green trees. It came via Ellis Island, heartbreak, bad health, and pain.

The search for an easier life made some members of my father's large family go off to Chicago, into the heartland of the Middle West. Before them there had been other Jews taking this same route, with wagons, horses, and their huddled energies, spreading their arts and crafts toward the West. But we remained on Cherry Street, content with having a great river as our neighbor. On Cherry Street everybody knew everybody. There were no strangers, Gentile or Jewish. And my mother could talk Russian to Russians, Polish to Poles, and Yiddish to our own. But whatever Cherry Street was, it was no bargain for anybody on the block. If you worked twice as hard as the next man you would soon transform yourself into a normal American immigrant on your way to everywhere and nowhere.

What had brought them all to Cherry Street and the other

17

ghettos? Tsarist persecution, anti-Semitism, impossible old worlds, conceits about the New World—as well as a mishmash of feelings and relationships. My father had never seen a pogrom, though, after he left Russia, a relative was killed in the Kishinev pogrom of 1903. My father had left because he got tired of being a conscript soldier and of being beaten, scarred, and humiliated. Russia had lost a war to Japan; a revolution had taken place in 1905; and, as usual, the Jews became the scapegoats of the *pogromchiks*—the tsarist-inspired hordes who murdered the Jews. Eight hundred and ten Jews were killed and 1,770 were wounded. After that, the Jewish immigrants arrived at Ellis Island in droves. In 1906, 150,000 Jews migrated to New York.

The Jews, believing that God's ways, though mysterious, would nevertheless protect them—fled from Russia, and Cherry Street, one of a hundred blocks to receive these new hordes of immigrants, was fully and finally settled as a ghetto within a cosmic, freewheeling nation. In fifteen years, between 1899 and 1914, more than a million and a half immigrants came to Ellis Island—and most remained in New York.

Our home was a little bit of Russia made by my father as a self-taught carpenter. The beds, for the children, formerly triple-tiered, gave way to American bedding, especially to the iron folding cots and beds that every Jewish household hid behind doors or in corners. In the center of the living room was a huge table with the breathing, bubbly samovar. A gas mantle, the white webbing encasing the gas jet, burned above it. In the kitchen, which consisted mostly of a tub, a huge stove, a round table, and us, was a gas meter. Over the stove was a water boiler. The tub, which had been built for washing clothes, was used for our weekly bath before the Sabbath or when we were not being rushed down to Rutgers Street Public Bath with towels and soap. We lived between bits and pieces of two countries, the mixture serving to fuse and confuse us all the more.

As children, we were American-grained from the start. But to our parents we were always Jews, never American, though we lived within a perplexing set of physical and spiritual nuances.

18

Our Jewishness came with the preparation for the Sabbath. It meant going to the bakery with a ten-pound iron pot filled with meat and vegetables, the *tsholnt*. The pot cover was tightly sealed to keep all the odors in the pot, and I was usually the one in our family who carried it to the bakery on Monroe Street—a sweaty, flour-laden place operated by a family of four. They baked and they shouted. They were down to their underwear at the back of the bakery, shoving the pots into the huge hot recesses of the baking oven. There the pots remained for twenty-four hours, baking slowly; and there I would go back after Saturday's morning service, to take the hot pot back home for the best meal of the week. My mother blessed the *khale*—the Sabbath bread—over the candles still burning from Friday; my father blessed the wine, and all of us turned to the *tsholnt*, awaiting the pot's exotic revelations. The slow cooking of the *tsholnt* was always done at the bakeries—we could not do it at home, and nobody ever did.

All these acts were ritualistic. Like the coming of the *shabes goy* to turn off the gas mantle on Saturday or to light the stove and heat something for our big feast. On the Sabbath only a Gentile boy or man, the *shabes goy*, was allowed to do that.

The drinks, too, were ritualistic. My father, an old Russian hand at religious-type bootlegging, made kvass, a scarcely alcoholic beverage made from stale bread, as well as schnapps, mead, and beer. During the week, since he worked twelve hours a day, he had his schnapps on coming home. We watched him sip it, turn red in the face, cough, roll a cigarette, ask what damage I had done that day—and then sink into dinner. It might be fish, borscht with meat and potatoes, or a stew, always with black bread, tea. Then he turned to his Jewish newspapers.

During the week he was worn out. On the Sabbath he glowed. During the week he was the presser of cloaks, standing on his badly varicosed legs, pushing a ten-pound pressing iron. It was piecework from factory to factory; from Greene Street up to Seventh Avenue. The factories made religious Jews turn to Socialism, anarchism, and unionism in those harrowing deadly

19

days before World War One. And on the Seventh Day, as he filled a thimble full of schnapps for all the children and my mother, he rested. . . .

He was to vote Socialist often, though occasionally for a Democrat, depending on whether the candidate was Jewish. He voted racially, as did most Jews on the Lower East Side; and, good union member that he was, he went to meetings regularly on East Broadway, or to his Bialystoker Sick and Death Benefit Society, named after his native province of Bialystok and meeting over the burlesque show on East Houston Street. He read all the newspapers, mostly Hebrew and Yiddish, that my mother sold from her newsstand at the synagogue on Madison Street . . . and he would, on occasion, grin while reading.

My mother would ask, "What is so funny, Berel?"

"Nothing is funny, Chai-Sura. Everything is tragic everywhere . . ." yet he was smiling, hiding some private joke, turning pages of *The Forward, The Journal, The Tageblatt, The Stick*—papers that had a variety of political outlooks and, one of them, *The Forward*, later reached a peak of 220,000 readers. Today, with only three of them remaining, *The Forward* has 75,000 readers. My father is no longer one of them.

"You can vote," I said one day, forcing him into embarrassment. "A big letter came today. You are a citizen, Father."

"I am a citizen?" He smiled whimsically. "After all these years? I must vote?"

"*Got zol ophitn*—a citizen *nokh* (God forbid—a citizen yet)!" went my mother. "How much money did that cost you that you don't have? Is God a citizen?"

"Money like that cannot be counted, Chai-Sura. I must vote, of course. God does not vote in America. . . ."

"For whom will you vote?"

"For Meyer London, of course. . . ."

"Not for Dickstein?" said my mother. "He wears glasses too, Berel."

My father voted for a man he believed looked even more distinguished, Meyer London, a Socialist with glasses, who ran

20

for various offices. I had taught him enough English to pass the literacy test. I had taught him how to sign his name—but in the area of politics he was so knowledgeable that there was nothing that I could tell him about Socialist and Democratic politics on the East Side.

"Did God tell you how to vote? Did the rabbi?" asked my mother. "If you're looking for yesterday—you won't find it today."

"Voting is not one of God's problems. As for the rabbi, let him be the good Jew and teach us God's ways and not democracy," answered my father, rolling another cigarette.

My mother never voted. She had piety, not literacy—she believed in more God, more faith, more charity. These were enough, then, to give her immortality and to make a family grow up on Cherry Street.

Our folkways were based on daily verbal festivals. We talked a blue streak in Yiddish about everything. The radio had not reached us, though some neighbors had a crystal set, with earphones—and they would occasionally call us in to listen to strange voices crystallizing from a black box made of Bakelite on some tubes burning brightly. My mother listened and said that it was God, of course. The telephone was also God's work. So was Seltzer water, for getting the gas out of your stomach. So was the schnapps, that made some men *shikker* down in the saloons—the Irish and the Poles, but not the Jews, who never went into the cellar saloons off the corner of Gouverneur Slip. And despite all the festivals we had on holidays or when relatives and friends visited, no one ever got *shikered* (drunk) in my father's flowing house. There tea took the place of too much schnapps; and *lekakhs*, a brown honeycake, went with the fruit and the diverse talk.

Our folkways also included a warning song, "*Shikker iz a goy vayl er iz a goy.*" (As long as a man is a non-Jew, he's a drunk.) It was a song from Russia and Poland used against the *pogromchiks*, and it had a mocking racial air. You laughed, felt superior —being nonalcoholic—and you went on to other rational matters.

21

Goy, then, was as much a word denoting a possible Christian drinker who might drink too much as it was a word merely denoting a Christian. Today, in retrospect, with many cheap ironies being used for galling twists in linguistic humor, I am hardly able to appreciate racial jokes, nor Jewish comics, nor rabbis turned professional comedians. But in those days we were just Galicians and Litvaks—able to laugh at each other. You laughed and you laughed! In England it must be the same between a Yorkshireman and a man from Lancashire.

For reasons that were as much physical as psychological, sickness among Jews had a high ratio then. They were strangers, aliens, Jews—who'd always been preyed on. In those days, the small fat man or the tall thin man with the goatee and the black bag who walked up to the fifth floors of our tenements, must have taken the Hippocratic Oath seriously. The doctor came. He had his basic equipment. Your lungs, your heart, your fever, your sores, your eyes, your throat—whatever your trouble, the visits all cost a dollar or less, with the medicine. If you did not have the dollar you owed him a dollar. The doctor, too, came from the same *gegent*, or district. He was a *landsman*. He had been a neighbor in another country. He knew the history of your kith and kin. He was an honored man, then. He healed. We believed in doctors, for they were like the rabbis. They smoked. They smelled of tobacco. They were tired all the time—and when they visited, they were soon drinking a glass of tea and eating some Sabbath cake.

The visit of the doctor was as social as it was medical. We usually got better and without psychological overtones. Up at three and four and off to work, we were too harried to conceive of anything psychiatric in our myth-laden midst. We had God, we knew. After God, or before, there was no one with whom one could talk anything over except the dollar doctor, a man related in a thousand ways to our past, especially on the strident, hectic Lower East Side.

Accidents were always with us. When I was six my mother was run over by an ice truck. She had crawled beneath it to pick up some fallen pieces of ice—a habit of poverty to keep the food we had from spoiling. The truck ran over her right shoulder. Her right arm was amputated . . . and we were amputated, with permanent grief. She was fifty-one then, and went on selling newspapers, and taking care of us.

Horses kicked you as you patted them. We were clumsy with horses, though they were then on the way out, as electric cars purred with increasing frequency along the dirty streets. Horses, dirt, mobs of kids—everything and everybody took to the middle of the street, and accidents were the natural result. The sidewalks were for stands selling fruit, newspapers, shirts, and old clothes. The gutters, where dead horses lay for days or until a special truck came along to haul the horse off, were most of our playgrounds.

"Horses have nothing to do with God," said my wisdom-laden mother. "Nor do dogs, cats, and rats. They *peyger* (perish like dogs, without an afterlife). . . ."

I used to insist that horses and animals were like human beings, but somewhat dumb. Many of my friends were just as dumb though they talked forever about everything and nothing. A cat was a cat. A dog was a dog. An animal *peygered*. Did animals suffer? My mother doubted that animals suffered. Jews suffered, she was certain. There was sickness. There was sin. There was death . . . and in our home there were no animals—not even cockroaches, we were so clean.

Animals suffered. I knew. There was that cat that I had thrown into the East River off Corlears Hook Park, to teach the cat how to swim. It swam, but back to me. Did I want to drown the little cat? I wanted the cat to do what I could not do—to swim to the Brooklyn Navy Yard, just across the river. Instead, the cat drowned—and I suffered for years after that. Today, when most of my friends are cat lovers, cat dander plays havoc with my nose, and, without doubt, my floating subconscious.

Half heathen that I was in my mother's eyes, I cried over the drowned cat. It meowed into my dreams, and the Brooklyn Navy Yard howled in my dreams. That cat, a stray without a

23

HARRY ROSKOLENKO

tag, with no special color, just pure cat, turned me into an amateur lover of animals. It made me take to nature and eventually
to the wilderness, all over the world.

We knew about death as children learn about death. Death
came to sick people. Death came from accidents, horses, trucks,
broken heads, cops' clubs, gang fights—and sickness. But only
the old died, we thought. Death was for the aged, a phantom
without a calling card. When one of our young died, we thought
it strange, hardly in keeping with God's design and will.

My sister Esther was killed by a truck at the age of fifteen.
Elsewhere I have written about the accident but not much about
Esther. She was the oldest of the then-six children. She was
all glow, most beautiful—on her way to becoming a *femme fatale*.
She worked as a salesgirl at Hearns on Fourteenth Street. She
walked the two miles to the store in the morning, a book and
some sandwiches in her arms, and she would read her book in
Union Square during her lunch. She had no particular gifts
except her beauty—dark, Russian, and Semitic. She was all
smiles, warmly affectionate with my one-year-old brother Bill,
called Velvel; always hugging the pink baby, talking about making a middy blouse, helping my one-armed mother get the house
in order—and she was killed by a truck that belonged to Hearns
as she was walking down Lafayette Street on her way home.

Who knew about lawyers? What we knew, we got—a shyster,
called so by all of us Jews and for basic reasons. In those days
some lawyers had just begun to chase ambulances—to gear up
their law practices. My mother found one without much of a
practice. Some years later, five hundred dollars was given to her
for my sister's death. What the lawyer got—the lawyer knew. We
never found out.

"What is there to find out? The ways of the law outside of
the synagogue?" asked my mother.

All those accidents! I often wonder how any of us, though
agile enough to escape getting our heads broken daily, managed
to live through our growing-up days. Gas explosions occurred
regularly in the tenements. People fell down open elevator shafts.

24

The wooden floors of the tenements fell in. Fire escapes broke, flinging sleepers into the streets. There were terrible fires.

I was the permanent witness to pain at home. My father was locked into a freezer at Wilson & Company. My father was hit by bricks—almost losing an eye. On the outside, the fights between the gangs were routine—and often they occurred on the quiet Sabbath. Then Jews were attacked because they were Jews. A bearded man, or one with a yarmulke, would not dare walk down certain streets. A democratic civil war went on continually all over the Lower East Side.

Gangs and politicians went together. Tammany Hall had its gangs—for Election Day routines. Each block had its fighting gang, taking in everybody. It was pure block kinship—disregarding origin, speech patterns, and religion. The gangs were nations unto themselves . . . and when we fought each other, we acted as early heralds of darkness on the American soil. Years later, in Spanish Harlem, the gangs were to fight over their *turf*, over their girls, over their alleged cultural differences, including the color of their skin.

In our day the fighting was seldom about religion, except when it came to the Jews. Then we were suddenly Jews—they Christians. The saloons, always open, and too many to a block, brought out the drunken fighters. Who did not get a beating in those primitive days after the turn of the century? Women, children, strangers—and even cops.

Occasionally I would go to meet my father up at Wilson & Company, the slaughterhouse. It was a long walk to First Avenue and 38th Street. But I did not walk. I hitched rides on the trolleys—for no kid ever paid his way when he could hitch it. Once at Wilson & Company, I would find my father deep in blood and slaughtered sheep. I was there to see him because I had a letter from Russia that looked as if it needed an immediate reply.

I saw the sheep and I saw the endless rivers of blood. Behind a gate was the ram, the Judas goat. Behind other gates were the sheep. Down a dirty track he led all of them . . . and I would

25

say, "Papa, how can you do this? Does God know what happens at the end of the track?"

"He knows, son. There is no other job here or over in New Jersey for a Jew. . . ."

Poles, Swedes, and the Irish worked there at Wilson & Company. They slaughtered for the Gentiles, not for Jewish rituals. What was my father doing there among all the Gentiles? They thought he was a whole Russian, not a Jew.

"What does the letter say?" I asked.

"It's from Gidalya—Mama's half brother. He wants to come to America. He has four sons and a wife and they are hungry, he says. I will call a family meeting for Sunday. . . ."

On Sunday, they came—a mob, all of them relatives. My mother would tell me who they were—for the tenth time. When they left, I forgot them again. Who was the fat woman with the skinny husband? Who was the man with the bulging gold teeth? Who was the short woman with the gold watch on a chain over her big bosom? Who was the one with the gray wig? Who was everybody and anybody? They were uncles, cousins, and aunts in a glorified Gilbert and Sullivan opera, Russian-Jewish style.

They crowded into the living room. They stood. They sat on the floor and window sills. They ate herring and black bread. They drank up all the homemade schnapps, kvass, and mead. Nothing was left but words, promises, some torn dollars that were pushed over to my father—all entered into a ledger.

Somehow, within a year, Gidalya arrived. Later his wife and their four sons came. It was all very simple from the herring and the schnapps to bring a new greenhorn, often called, when angry, a *maki*, a *griner*, or a *griner tukes* (a green ass) to Cherry Street. When Gidalya came, my father told me to take him to the baths on Rutgers Street for two hours, "so he does not bring Russian lice and the ship's lice into the house."

We knew the seasons the way we knew God in the synagogue, for the holidays denoted the weather in our souls. Spring meant joy. Summer's heat meant fire-escape sleeping, flies, bugs, the praying mantis, butterflies—and swimming bare-assed in the East River. Fall meant the harvest festival of Succoth, with a

26

beautiful little grass hut, in the back yard, that my father built to honor the gathering in of the crops. Around the little hut we ate and danced. There we sang Hebrew songs. There we left Cherry Street and went back thousands of grassy years. We thought of Moses in Egypt—and all the prophecies that my mother insisted would soon be fulfilled.

The seasons, too, had their patriotic holidays, with July 4th as the hottest and holiest of them all. Bonfires—great conflagrations. Speeches, along with rotten eggs. Stink bombs, along with patriotism. Brass bands. Noise. Cops acting kind on that day. But, when Columbus Day came, there was always an argument. Somebody said that Columbus was a Jew, wandering about like one. My mother merely said, "A curse to Columbus," with the traditional Yiddish *"A klug tsu Columbus!"* He had discovered America. But so had my father, born in 1860, coming four hundred years after Columbus. And all my father could say, when asked about Columbus Day, was, "I will not get paid for this *yontev* (holiday). A double *klug tsu Columbus!*"

Schooling in my time, at P.S. 31, was very stern. The teacher, though not a cop, was nevertheless a ruler-wielding teacher. We knew the ruler because it was often applied to our asses by both teacher and principal. We would get slapped, and they were right. I was never right at any time—said my parents, who were immediately told of each incident by a note from the teachers or the principal. They sided with the teachers, and my report card proved that I was sleeping when I should have been studying. I was *left back*—a phrase that became quite familiar around our house.

Besides going to the bakery and carrying important letters to my father, I had other chores, like getting up at three in the morning to help my mother at her newsstand. This chore did me no good at school; I slept and was slapped. I answered questions wrongly and was slapped. For every error, from spilling ink on girls' dresses to feeling their bottoms—I was slapped. Schooling, oddly, was very stern even when I was not getting slapped.

Nevertheless, all of us learned quickly. There was no easy route

27

to high school and college. We did not smoke or take dope, though opium was not exactly illegal. We saw the smokers in Chinatown or up on Sixth Avenue under the El and they were strange people. They had glassy eyes. They shook with palsy. None of us wanted drugs, nothing but ice-cream sodas and swimming at Coney Island.

When I asked my mother about opium, she shook her head.

"What is opium?" she asked.

"They put it into a pipe and smoke it in a hurry. . . ."

"I'll ask the rabbi about opium," was her next statement. "Do Jews smoke it?"

"Only the Chinese in Chinatown," I said.

"Then it's not God's or the rabbi's problem."

"Whose problem is it, Mother?"

"The Chinese, son."

Election time came with bands and orators without loudspeakers. The orators stood on hurriedly made platforms and shouted to us from cupped hands about poverty, working conditions, sweatshops and child labor. For the Socialist-minded Jews, there was always Meyer London, who lived on Grand Street and wore those fancy glasses my mother had mentioned. Obviously, his glasses made him a great man in our eyes. He had some special vision, we thought, as we listened to his Socialist explanations regarding our human situation.

Who was not a Socialist then in our midst? It was hard to conceive of a Jew who was a Republican, yet there were men like Dickstein, a Democrat, who always managed to get elected to Congress. After Meyer London there was Judge Jacob Panken, who, to my mind, merely had a first name called Judge. He was always being elected. As a Socialist with a heart, he gave out lighter sentences than many other judges. And there was the really great Socialist leader, Morris Hillquit, our Marx and Engels by Jewish fiat. We had not yet heard of Norman Thomas, although we knew of Eugene V. Debs.

The Socialists would do their best talking in Yiddish in front of *The Forward* building on East Broadway, up against Seward Park. It had to be Yiddish to get any sort of sympathetic listeners. Women in babushkas, just as they wore them in Russia and Poland, listened and cried. Men, who from their appearance might just have come over from Warsaw and Lodz, looked stern, shaking their heads at what was happening to them. Twelve and fourteen hours a day. Lunch, about twenty minutes. Piecework, which meant self-slavery. Strikes. Cold factories. Hot factories. Airless traps. Fires, always fires. The 1911 fire at the Triangle Waist Factory, that killed 146 girls and women, was constantly referred to by organizers from the Amalgamated Clothing Workers Union and the International Ladies Garment Workers Union. The Socialism of panic was all over East Broadway.

Socialism, with its idealistic language, had special appeals for us Jews. After all, had it not come from Europe? But this was New York, corrupt and democratic, but with amazing energy. We could vote—and they could not vote in another country. There were no cossacks on horses whirling the *nagaika*. No Siberia, either. But it was capitalism terrorizing the working class, said Morris Hillquit, our leader—''so vote for Meyer London and Jacob Panken . . .''

When we talked about Socialism at home, it was more through the use of symbols than from actual knowledge. Had my father read Marx? He'd heard of him. Had he known any Socialists in Russia? A few. Would he vote for a Socialist who was not Jewish? He looked puzzled—then said no. It was Yiddish Socialism with East Broadway, his sick and death benefit society, his membership in the Union. It was Socialism over a glass of tea with lemon on a side dish.

Who wasn't poor in those days? When poverty included 80 percent of the people on the Lower East Side, it lost its private meaning. It was there for all. Of course, we had charities for the really poor and the sick. Children without fathers or sad-looking orphans received special attention. Jewish orphans? That was too much for my mother, who immediately started collecting for them. She had dozens of *pushkes* in the kitchen closet. The

29

pushkes were the little boxes made of tin, with openings small enough for nickels and pennies. They were charity boxes—emptied every week by a little old man with a black bag—and many an orphan who became a doctor is indebted to my mother for at least one month of his medical education. But it was the Jewish Socialists, who were not the most religious of men, who rallied us instead to the then-pink Red Flag of municipal Socialism in the making.

By 1904, the Socialist Party had 20,000 members. It was, then, municipal Socialism, gradualism, and talk about the eventual disappearance of capitalism. There was, of course, the IWW, the Wobblies, which numbered few Jews among its members—and was named Wobblies by a Chinese cook who could not make his way through so tough a name as The Industrial Workers of the World.

In my father's time, from stories he told me later, he had not heard of the 1903 split in the Russian Socialist movement. As for the word "Bolshevik," it was first heard by him in 1917, when all of us heard of it on Cherry Street. It was a frightening word—with exploding bombs attached to it by most Socialists who opposed it. By 1918, when the Bolsheviks took over Russia, the revolution split the Socialist Party in the United States, and many friends and families also split over the issue.

By 1908, when my father had been in New York for thirteen years, and was attending Socialist mass meetings, the Socialist Party in the United States had doubled its membership. It had 2,500 locals in the country. It flooded through the East Side, from synagogues to unions. It had its great proselytizers, men like Abraham Cahan, the novelist-editor of *The Forward*. My father liked the gradualism of Abraham Cahan and the social ideas of Morris Hillquit, the Party's theoretician, who said in 1910, when my father walked the picket line during the great Cloakmakers Strike, "Our principal efforts must be directed towards the propaganda of Socialism among the workers. But they should by no means be limited to that class alone. . . . The ultimate aims of the movement far transcend the interests of any

30

one class in society, and its social ideal is so lofty that it may well attract large numbers of men and women from other classes. . . . [The workers] are by no means the only class which has a direct economic motive for favoring a change of the existing order. . . ."

Under these all-inclusive words, my father, good Jew that he was, hard working every day, was a Socialist.

I remember my father telling me, a few years later, on a Sunday, of a meeting he had gone to in 1910 to hear Debs at the Hippodrome.

"Debs spoke. What did I understand in English? Almost *gornisht* (nothing). But there must have been ten thousand people there. It smelled like my old barn used to smell—from animal *drek*."

Socialism, Judaism, concerned parents, and the local boys' clubs, kept the errant among us somewhat straight. Since Cherry Street, where a half-dozen model tenements were put up in 1887, did not have a settlement house, we went to Madison House and the Henry Street Settlement for games of play that kept us from mass mayhem in the streets.

The Neighborhood Playhouse on Grand Street was then about to start its exercises in dramaturgy and make some of us actors, poets, playwrights, and spectators, as we saw the great English classics for the first time in our culture-hungry lives. But it was the Educational Alliance, a massive building on East Broadway, four blocks from my home, that was to have the major portion of our youthful allegiance. There we became gymnasts—to tumble our way onward. We became Boy Scouts, to camp overnight in the Palisades, quite a frontier of rocks in 1916 when I was nine, with a Hudson River you could swim in, and with rattlesnakes that you impaled with a stick. When you got your first snake, you were definitely an all-around American Boy Scout ready to tame the rest of the nearby American wilderness.

The Educational Alliance gave us what we could not learn at school, in a setting created for energetic scholarship. The Alli-

31

ance, formerly known as the Hebrew Institute, supported by wealthy American Jews, set up the huge building at Jefferson Street and East Broadway in 1893. It was the intellectual heart of the Jewish ghetto. And there I could write my early poetry, have it read, then laughed at by my friends all the way home through the dark, dirty streets. The Alliance Art School was founded by the painter Henry McBride. There, earlier and later, men like Jacob Epstein had come to sculpt; and members of the eventual school of realism-cum-proletarianism had their basic education there with live models. There, too, some ranking artists of the modern era studied—Leonard Baskin, Peter Blume, Adolph Gottlieb, Chaim Gross, Ben Shahn, and William Zorach. For the Education Alliance was an intellectual and moral testing ground for those not about to become antisocial gangsters and killers. Years later, students of mayhem and murder were to enroll in other alliances like Murder Incorporated.

The Educational Alliance made some of us boxers, as well. There were Benny Leonard, Sammy Sieger, Sid Terris, Ruby Goldstein, Charley Rosen, Barney Ross, Terry Roth, Lou Kersch, Johnny Clinton—who always carried a Yiddish newspaper in his pocket. Boxing, then, was the way to the top, American style. It was, then, as Jewish as it was Italian and Irish, with few Negroes able to get past the managerial edifice, to slash their way upward.

But most of us worked after school at diverse jobs for a nickel an hour. I rolled empty milk cans for Breakstone & Levine, then starting out in business across from my house, at 365 Cherry Street. There was Breakstone, in a white coat, and Levine, in a dirty coat, checking 50-pound tubs of butter; sour milk cans, pure cream cans, pot cheese pots—and for a nickel an hour we got the containers into the freezers in the back, taking a little cheese away with us for home use to help fill out the black bread, the herring and potatoes, and the thick meat borscht that was always on tap.

My two older brothers, Mike and Herschel, were a different sort; for my mother soon taught them the value of a trade to make real money. By the time they were fourteen and sixteen they had learned all there was to a new American trade—soda jerking, which they picked up after school at Marchiony's Italian ice-cream parlor on Grand Street.

My mother had a passion about success, American style. It was in the streets, easy to find. All that a boy or a man had to do was to seize the opportunity. It was not garbage, if you worked it over. It was for the sons of immigrants who were willing to apply themselves to stuff the American dream with the dollars of success . . . and with my mother as a suddenly inspired banker, my two older brothers by the time they were, respectively, eighteen and sixteen, already had a future.

She had saved $1500 for them from their earnings. She gave them fifty cents a week to spend recklessly; the rest of their earnings she used to buy a partnership in a luncheonette on Duane Street and Broadway. Soon they bought out their Greek partner and he went off to Lesbos to retire among the olive groves. The cash logic of the purchase was all very simple for my mother, who told us: "Don't work for others. Work for yourself. Don't be like your father, a wage slave. . . ."

They became millionaires. They bought restaurants, developed them, sold them. Herschel, the oldest, became the *gevir*—rich enough by all the values crowding us off the American earth. It was to be a traditional success story—a *mayse*, told over and over again on the Lower East Side

Who was not a wage slave on the East Side? But with World War One everything changed in value, price, and wages. My brother, Herschel, even before the luncheonette, had gone off to the Hog Island Shipyards, to become a riveter and hold the Hog Islanders together. Later, as a sailor, I was to live on these ships for seven years. Herschel, liberated at age thirteen, was making three times as much as my father was, still sweating over a pressing iron, unable to rivet, too old to change his trade, too tired to transform himself into any sort of storekeeper, entrepreneur, war profiteer, rag merchant, or shortage specialist.

There was money in the streets, at last. America was at war

33

and President Wilson said it was "to make the world safe for democracy." America was no longer a thief. But among the cynical Socialists and anarchists, many of them in jail, it was a war "to save the capitalistic Democratic Party. . . ."

My mother lamented for my future. I was warned too late. I had read the English classics. Byron decided my destiny along with a Russian named Pushkin. Further, I had the wrong sort of friends to think of working in an ice-cream parlor. I had also been liberated, at ten, by the war and its outcome. My official Judaism ended with my Bar Mitzvah, a last concession to my family. I was hardly the Jew my father was. I was hardly my father's son, as well, in my interests. My friends, in their fashion, were breaking all their own ties with rigorous Judaism. A few were reading German philosophy, especially Schopenhauer. Poetry went with pessimism, I was soon to find out. It did not go with joy, I was to learn forever. My four good friends, who made up a circle of boy writers, thinkers, adventurers—as strong in body as they were then muscular with grand thoughts—were all to go on from Cherry Street.

The synagogue meant nothing to me after thirteen, though Judaism is still my private world. Long fascinated with rivers, at thirteen I ran away to sea, after an argument with my father, following with my whole self the eye that had gazed across the Hudson. I never went back to school for long, but remained a reader of books, because I had to read to know. Pagan almost; then Marxist. Marxism replaced the phylacteries that I left one day in a barn. And, some years later, Marxism was to go as well —along with other self-delusions about the social nature of man.

As I was growing up, my mother in anger would say to me after some errant adventure, "You act like a *goy*. You will *peyger* like a *goy*. That *meshugene* (crazy) river! Where does it flow? Through your *narisha kop* (foolish head)? Through your books? *A po-et vilstu zayn? Mit vos—mit narishkayt?*" (A poet you want to be? With what—with your foolishness?)

My friends did not become boxers, businessmen, or gangsters, but that other thing—the *narishkayt mentshn* (foolish people).

34

One foolish friend became a professor of English literature and a specialist on Henry James; a second became a scientist, specializing in mathematical values; a third, a social historian; a fourth, once a famous editor, soon became a Soviet spy, to specialize in another form of *narishkayt*. I became, in time, a poet for seven books, as well as the revolutionary organizer, a prophet for the new order. By the time I was sixteen, I was a Marxist-cum-Trotskyite when I sailed in the black gang and on deck through the political and physical seas around the world.

In an earlier book, *When I was Last on Cherry Street*, much of my family's history appears. In poems written years after, I am still the kid running away. I am within the strictures of my Judaic upbringing. I am dreaming of sexual adventures. I am, endlessly, the sentimental boy and man, afraid of the lyricism we have lost and frightened by what we have gained in our American growth—a megalopolis, in stone and people.

I left the East Side and came back as a yearly visitor, to note all the changes—the high-rises making a more anonymous world of the new tenements. The East River still flows by. The Brooklyn Bridge, with its skeletal, Hart-Cranean mystique, is still there—to numb us with its frames of meaningful creation. One world has gone. Another, less giving, all concrete, flows up yearly. I have a major lament for the death of my father's world and his time. The death of that world is permanent and will never be reborn in our massive rush to Nothingness. Death is a tombstone that is often not engraved . . . but I write my own signature to our 1971 preview of hell. . .

When I was a Trotskyite, from 1927 to 1938, I could hardly believe that Trotsky was a poor sort of Jew, and, much worse, a former commissar. What Stalin did Trotsky would have done, had he remained in power. The theoretical differences did not really change their basic philosophy of how to keep Russia under a Communist dictatorship.

A man changes all the time. It is like his body. How does one grow up? What does one give up? You drop your romantic views,

35

in time. You take up things that are easier on your spirit, your dreams, your future. Is there one? There was one—when I was much younger. There is still the City that houses me—the poured concrete that God did not create for us. The green things of my youth are gone . . . and we live within a contemporary vacuum.

I preferred to escape our *growth*—and I long ago gave up this concrete world. My resignation included many things that are materialistic but few things of the spirit. It included organized Judaism. I am not organized for anything now. Poverty will always be here—and I have accepted it for myself. My few ambitions mostly deal with writing, with going to desolate places, with waters—alone. God is there for me. I do not need choruses on the Sabbath; nor *Yisker* (prayer for the dead), to lament for my parents; nor *Yom Kippur* to lament for what we were and what we have become. I lament alone.

I was, even in my Marxist days, the odd man—a Trotskyite, when almost everybody was a Stalinist. I was a Jew who went to sea, when others went to factories, shops, and Madison Avenue. I was the muscular poet of the revolution among thin poets. I was the wanderer, looking for desolate places to take me away from the original images of Cherry Street, East Broadway, Delancey Street—and Judaism. I had, I learned, become the Marxist so as not to be the Jew—the permanent scapegoat I thought that my father was. I did not have side curls. Today, when Judaism is often a sentimental awareness of differences and the memory of pain and the past, I am the Jew all the time. But then I hated the symbolical uniform that the *frume Yid* (the ultrareligious) adopted. "God is in your heart, not in a uniform," I used to tell my mother.

"Is God in a long black satin coat?" I would ask my mother. "Is God in a wide fur hat?" Is God within a woman shaving off her hair as the good religious Jewish woman did? Why all this stupid separation? We were in America, free, with jobs. The Jews had broken out of their mental and physical ghettos—almost at will. We were not Negroes—and they were the saddest-happiest people—for they had a permanent identity

36

as very old Americans. Did I like them? Yes—why not? They laughed. They cried. They sang. They came from Africa—and we were almost neighbors thousands of years ago. They were separated by their color—and we by our pretensions toward a vague spiritual purity.

"Who chose us for what, Mother?" I would ask. "Why this ridiculous separation in clothes, customs, and habits of another time? Did God create these habiliments and give them to Moses too?"

"If the Jews do not separate themselves, they will be lost forever—intermarried,". my mother would say. "They cannot merge their hearts, my son. They cannot fuse Judaism with *goyishe* paganism. . . ." and paganism, to her mind, soon became the word *peyger* when she was critical of my ideas.

"We were chosen by Abraham, Jacob, and Isaac—and by Moses. For what? To go back to *Eretz Yisroel*—for our purity, my son . . ."

Our purity consisted of many things. One day, the land of Israel—*Eretz Yisroel*. It was an illusion, we knew. Who believed? Zionists and Orthodox Jews believed. Did I then? Hardly. It was a needed myth, an essential myth for Zionists, I thought—then. Socialism was easier to believe in. There were hundreds of thousands of American workers voting Socialist. The Balfour Declaration had not yet been "declared." My father, voting Socialist, believed, however, in the myth of *Eretz Yisroel*. I believed in myself—young, indestructible, combative, verging on atheism, suspecting all the appeals of Judaism, especially of Gan Eden. There was no heaven on Cherry Street, but lots of hell, and I was getting it in heavy doses, daily, as I matured by the minute.

I remember, when I was ten, stealing an apple from a fruit-stand. We had bushels of apples at home sent to us by Uncle David from his farm at Accord, New York. Uncle David had remained the farmer, moving from the Ukraine to New York City. Using the money he got from the sale of his farm in the Ukraine, he returned to the soil in Accord, where land, then, was cheap—and possessed what most immigrants, including my father, dreamt of but never attained. In Accord, David had horses, chickens—and apples. He died at the age of ninety-seven, an oak of a Jew. But despite David's apples, I had stolen an apple from an old woman at the fruitstand. I confessed to my father.

"How much can I, now a *goy*, confess?" I finally managed to ask, dodging a third slap. "It was just an apple, Papa."

"A thief is a thief!"

"They are God's apples," I said, turning everything around.

"They were God's apples until they reached the tree. Do you understand, *meshumed*?" *Meshumed* meant a convert to Christianity. I was hardly a convert to anything but my inner Judaic self.

"It is Socialism on the tree," I answered, baffling myself and my father by this strange conceit.

"*Nar! Meshumed! Peyger!*"

Called a fool, a Christian convert, and told to die like a dog, was now part of my father's permanent rebuke . . . and it was to grow worse within three years, soon after I was thirteen, when I had my head literally opened up by my father's strange anger at my questing inquiries.

I struck back and I ran, making the irreparable break, to the sea that was then the focus of all my imagination. It was my last defeat, and my first, if final, victory over my father. I had struck back—and I was no longer his Jewish son. I was a radical. All the signs were there. I was the poet using my own fists to defend the boy becoming the man—but I was running, leaving God behind along with my family; leaving a home to become the traveler to other worlds. My broken skull made me the total atheist as God leaked out of my bleeding head.

My father died at seventy-seven, in 1937—just before another war broke up the world. Before his death he was to move from Cherry Street to the Bronx and then to Brooklyn. He went to *shul* every day after he retired. He stayed longer. He prayed more. He wondered more. And he was to say to me one day in

THE TIME THAT WAS THEN

1937, "Son, I am dying. My left arm . . . my chest . . . my head
. . . my feet." He was as thin and pale as the death now feather-
ing his mind. He would still roll a Russian cigarette, smoke it
slowly, tears coming, then talk about old dead friends. Socialism
meant nothing but a name to him anymore. He had stopped
voting at seventy, saying, "Enough! Enough! Does it matter
who is elected? They are all thieves, Jewish and Gentiles alike.
Please, son, roll me another cigarette. Please find the cognac.
It helps a little bit. Please stay for supper. I never see you, son
. . . you are always running to those crazy political meetings.
Are you writing something that I would like to hear—something
about the *alte gegent* (the old neighborhood) or about God?"

He had died, actually, years before 1937, over a pressing
iron, in his unions, meeting halls, Second Avenue benefits societies, his *vereins*—and in his Zareby Koscielne memories. He was
hardly an American by his habits. He had elected a few Socialists—and he was never to know that Israel was to become a state.

My mother died during the Christmas of 1949 while I was in
London. A cable from my religious young brother, Bill, said:
"Mother died yesterday . . ." I had seen her a month before.
She was seventy-nine, blind, and in a nursing home. The wealth
of my brothers kept her there with other old Jewish women.
Someone fed her. Other old women talked with her. She smiled,
stroked my face, cried a little bit, called on God for the end.
She remembered little then of Cherry Street, of Zareby Koscielne
and the blond woman who had come from there in 1895, at
twenty-five; who had known every tragedy and nothing of sin;
who was always with God, charity, good deeds, unable to ever
learn to read or write; too simple yet very skillful; who had made
my brothers do the things they did to become rich; who had
called me a *goy*, but had taught me so many universal values—
from charity to my own conception of faith in myself. But *Eretz
Yisroel*, one of her prophecies, was, to her, now a reality.

The Lower East Side still has its vestiges, old tenements about
to be bulldozed into high-rise city projects. The hundreds of
thousands of immigrants who came there have scattered into

39

HARRY ROSKOLENKO

American statistics. Between 1950 and 1960, two hundred thousand left those streets. They are now in the middle class in other parts of New York, Queens, New Jersey, and Westchester. They are in the working class, as well. It is another racial vista, with some exceptions on East Broadway, on streets that cannot hold out . . . an area of cultural ghosts.

Like Second Avenue, which bloomed on every corner with a Yiddish theater, a café, a cuisine that was as intellectual as *tsimes*, that old life is dead. Where the great Café Royale once was, there is a cleaning store, symbolic of the dry cleaning and the vacuum that have replaced Yiddish theaters, Yiddish characters, Yiddish poets, and playwrights—and the language itself. For the Café Royale, an establishment with a past as rich as Café Le Dome or Le Select on Montparnasse, was where all of us went during the twenties, thirties, and the forties. Instead of a *Yidishe* culture we have the illusion of values in cultural concrete pouring over people and places.

Yiddish culture is a ghost, though the sentimentality to recall it is awe-inspiring the more it disappears. It is like the Socialist Party and the men who built it—gone. It is like my relatives, evaporating into the vacuum that New York has become. Only yesterday I went to the funeral of Gidalya, my mother's half brother, whom my father brought over fifty years ago. He had lived in two houses—and he died at 300 Cherry Street, a city housing project. Three of his four children became in time what many of the sons of immigrants became—American businessmen. And one became a professor of sociology—to haunt his own immigrant past in Zareby Koscielne.

Chapter 2
The Boarder

He was, usually, lonely and bereft—a totally alien individual. He was a boarder, aged thirty—or any age; and he had a wife in Russia awaiting a *shifskart*. But he was a boarder living with a family in some kind of lackluster, ego-suffering relationship. He was tolerated, as a rule, merely for the money he paid out for a little back bedroom in a tight railroad-style flat.

The room was often windowless, or it opened onto another squat room that had a window on a yard. It was lit by gas or by a candle that the boarder bought. If he paid more than two dollars a week in rent, there might be a gas mantle to illuminate, with flickering drama, his goings and comings between his job and the synagogue. And if he was not religious, there was some obvious panic regarding his soul, his sins, and his immediate future as a boarder.

For out he went on his first trespass. The *baleboosteh* of the flat, an overworked, efficient, overly pregnant *froy*, would storm to her beleaguered husband—"Who needs this madman? He's dirty! He walks around as if he was in a Turkish bath! Naked, *nokh*! And when did he go to *shul* last? For a Jew he's more

41

like a Polack! What do we need him for? For his dirty two dollars a week and all the tea and strudel that he steals? He spits in the sink! He farts like a cow! His underwear is *farkakt*—just like a pig! Tell him to go! Tell him to send for his wife! Let her take care of this *griner khalyere*. Understand! Understand!''

The boarder, a man without his own home, lived within an impolite society as a nonequal. He was the most recent *griner* to begin with. He had an immigrant's knowledge of New York and its customs. And though he was, he thought, among his own folk and fellow Jews, he was on his own spiritually and physically. The only thing that he had was his clothes, his job, the back bedroom—and God.

And he had to be a moral man at all times. He could not, for instance, have a rendezvous with another woman. It would be shameful with a woman waiting for him, for the *shifskart*, and the few hundred dollars he was savagely saving, to bring her and his young children to America. One day that would happen. One day he would be on his way to Ellis Island—and another railroad flat on Madison Street would be full of even more recent greenhorns. But here he was, boarding out, agitated by everything, happy to be off to work—for work meant the *shifskart*—but unhappy to return. Once back, he would lock himself in his back room and listen. His hosts were tearing him apart again. They were critical of his green ways, his clothes, his mendacity. He was, he knew, a boarder in an amateur insane asylum.

He became, in time, part of the folklore of Yiddish humor, Yiddish plays, and Yiddish musical comedies; every season had a song about the *griner cuzine*. In these pithy extravaganzas, he was always the clumsy man. He was awkward in his mind and much worse with his old-country reflexes. When at last he managed to attune himself to New York, he was soon all things: the ambitious man, the secret lover, the villain, the plotter, the rapist, the robber of widows—and similar folklore ingredients. As the secret lover he had fathered the child his hostess, Mrs. *Baleboosteh*, was bearing. It was obvious, said the hissing neighbors when the child was born: ''Look, the child even has his nose and his eyes. *Oy vey iz mir!*''

42

He was, just as often, the secretly rich banker about to donate all of his wealth to any number of Jewish cultural institutions, beginning with the Educational Alliance. He was, it was rumored, the man behind any number of gifted violin students about to make their debuts at Carnegie Hall. He was the famemaker, the giving art patron, the *groise gevir*. But he was, really, the boarder, the dreamer-*griner* in the Yiddish pantheon of panic and prayer. He was also the *melamed*, the great teacher of the Talmud and the Kabbala. He was, among other things, the *nar*, who did not know how his feet grew. Overstated and understated, he was the completely green man who would never learn to make a living in New York; or he was, to the contrary, the charming fool from Chelm—once a real place but now a mythical Russian village—and he could do anything that was good or bad to everyone with whom he came in contact.

Between the folklore and the sociological fact, the boarder was a man caught between worlds—for economic and religious reasons. For if one goes back far enough, it is recorded that every Jewish immigrant family of this era at some time took in a boarder—and "took in" was the phrase for this indelicate relationship. It involved a strange man, the wife of another man, close quarters, children, the washing of intimate garments, making a stranger's bed, feeding him, and giving him the warmth of another home. It involved a personal intimacy given only to husbands—not to boarders. Between a few straight-running rooms, a bathroom—which did not include a tub or shower, but merely a toilet in the hall—it was as intimate as a bedroom and a family quarrel. It had all the sights and sounds of a *mikva*, the ritual cleansing bath for preparing a bride.

Where did all these boarders live? In every flat in the four- and five-floor tenements, which they helped to populate, en masse, as they turned the rookeries into Polish and Russian villages. Each street, though not literally, flew its spiritual pennants—assigned to accommodate their minds, bodies, accents, and strangeness. The rooms, at best, were ten feet long, eight feet wide, high in the ceiling, but low in every other architectural savagery. Yet, long or short, the tenants of these flats were the

43

animated new voyagers. The furniture was, obviously, American-made junk. The walls, the cabinets, the tables, however, had all the flavors of Eastern Europe. The tenants, boarders, and hosts actually lived in two cities—New York, and a place in Russia; each flat had its combined flavors, with the old dominating the still not-known new. And, to make things more quixotic, each street, with American, English, and Colonial-type names, added up to many other mysteries that made no sense to the boarders newly come from abroad. What, for instance, did Madison Street, two blocks away, mean to my mother?

She had many mishmash accents to overcome. Among her colorful accents, Madison Street became, when she pronounced it as best she could, *Medd-ee-sin Strit*. It was related to medicine, to doctors, and never to one of the signers of the Declaration of Independence. Monroe Street, to which we eventually moved as we were coming up in the world of woe and money, was even harder for my mother to pronounce. It came out as *Mom-roach Strit*. As for our own Cherry Street, the fruit for which the street was named was not even a known fruit to my mother, who knew nothing of American agriculture, though I was able, after a few years, to tell her that our block had been a cherry orchard around the year 1703.

It is difficult to imagine that today. Once colonial, once the heart of Olde New York, once the home of President Washington, in my time the mile-long street housed poor Italians, Jews, Irish, and Russians. It was a line of tenements, with pigeons racing over the roofs. It gave off sea smells, odors of tar, odors of Indian spices—and the smell of beer. For each block had so many saloons, per person; but then, the brewing and selling of beer was as old as Cherry Street itself. There had been, I told my mother, a Mr. Richard Sackett, a prime brewer for ye colonials straight off the British ships, on their way to fight the French and the Indians, farther north, in the Bronx. "God Save the King" had rung thousands of times through Cherry Street before 1776 and before the New boarders began to arrive.

The boarders around 1905, and later, fought for the immediate

44

green dollar and that was legal enough. If they were skilled artisans, and most were not, they earned a laborer's poor wage. They boarded and they hoarded—to begin their savage climb up the ramparts of American civilization.

Work meant discipline, money, wives, and children. An immigrant, living alone, preferred to work, with extra jobs always handy then. When a boarder was not at work, he was sleeping or in the synagogue, involved in his Old World simplicity of prayer and worship; for the synagogue was the only place where he could express his faith and his constant fears. He was alone with God and grace, or with other immigrants. In the synagogue, too, he could meet *landsleit*. Between periods of praying, he managed to ask questions, to gossip, to learn. Away from the Torah there was another reality. In the streets, he was between blood, stone, and God.

There were parks, when he wanted green things and the memory of Ukrainian villages. But most of the cows, horses, sheep, goats, and chickens had left Manhattan by the time I was a boy. In Central Park only birds and people walked on the grass. In Corlears Park, straight at the end of Cherry Street, one could sit on the piers and watch freighters, ferries, and sailing ships gliding by. There one caught both wind and wave and the smells of the Lower East Side, which were healthier then. It was human then in sounds and smells. You breathed the purer manure; and, when you really wanted to see cows, you went to Goldberg's Farm, not too far from Middle Village—the last Jewish farm in Brooklyn after we turned into the new century.

Our own boarder, Gidalya, was hardly a special kind, though he was related to us on my mother's side. He was average in all things—a religious Jew transplanted from a small place to a huge, noisy, difficult city. It was dirty from the horses; but then, his home villages had horses. Gidalya, however, was not interested in manure but in the money to bring his wife and four children over.

His working languages, when he arrived at Ellis Island, were,

like my father's, all non-English. We talked Yiddish amid the
mobs of immigrants in the red-bricked, panoplied entry building.
There Turks met Turks, Jews met Jews—and everybody was
either crying, laughing, or both.

We greeted Gidalya, as an about-to-be boarder, with familial
kisses, brotherly hugs, sisterly eyes—and questions, all of them
unanswered. All of our questions were smiled at: much as if the
only reflex working for an immigrant-*cum*-boarder was his smile,
as he looked at the Statue of Liberty. After all, he was a stranger
among us, who had written letters to my mother, his half sister.
They had never met before. And my mother, who had seen the
Statue of Liberty much earlier, had most likely smiled the same
way upon her arrival.

Gidalya, like my father, was never to learn English, though
Gidalya's son, Velvel, whom we soon called William, was to become a professor of sociology, with the kinship and choice of that
bizarre profession acutely related to William's immigrant past.
But the boarder, Gidalya, was no more concerned with American
sociology than he was with American-made manure. He was a
carpenter. He had built barns, houses, outhouses, pigpens,
chicken coops—in another country; but now, in New York, soon
very much at home in my father's crowded house, he was,
nevertheless, mostly a shy man. His half sister, my mother, was
as strange to him as we were. He was a lonely man, yet whimsical,
when he had one holiday drink, which was more than enough to
bring out the alien and the boarder. Then he became tender to us;
for we constantly reminded him of his own children in a village
in the Ukraine. He was forever saying, "To have been born
here is a blessing . . ." We had, he assured us, been very very
lucky to have been born on Cherry Street.

Gidalya had his saw trade, but he was never to become a member of the carpenter's union. For membership was handed down
from father to son in those guild-type craft-union days . . . and
I remember seeing Gidalya on a wintry day, hatted for a Siberian
New York climate, standing with his gunnysacked saw, looking
for a boss carpenter to hire him for a day's freezing work.

Before World War One, carpenters in the city stood on selected street corners. Soon someone officious, looking a bit cleaner, would arrive. They were contractors, boss carpenters, builders of stores, renovators—changing the earlier business face of the slums. The jobs lasted a day or a week. The price was bargained for; but if a man needed a day's work badly, he would compete, cut the price, ashamed, offering himself up for less than his fellow carpenters . . . and soon that corner would become untenable for him.

Daily, when Gidalya returned, he would tell us what he had built during those twelve hours in Siberian weather.

"A store front," he said in Yiddish.

"For what?" asked my mother.

"For dry goods on Riv-ink-tun."

"What kind of dry goods?" went my mother.

"Dry dry goods," I said.

"*Khokhem fun Chelm*," said my mother. "How much did they pay you?"

Gidalya took out three dirty dollars.

"In Zareby it would have taken a week, Chai-Sura," said Gidalya, pleased with his sudden wealth.

The next day he was doing holier work, repairing benches at my father's synagogue on Madison and Montgomery.

"Too many *melameds* are tearing their pants. They complain," said my father. "Use glue, not nails . . ."

"Glue, nails, pants, *melameds*. Let them stick to the benches," added my mother, feeling holier.

Another day, Gidalya made racks for a bookstore on East Broadway. He brought home a tattered book—*The Call of the Wild*. He handed it to me. My first introduction to Jack London, it was to change the pattern of my life.

"What is it all about?" asked my mother.

I tried to explain a few days later.

"*Vilde fleysch?* What do you need such a book for? You're wild enough without that book."

The wild bodies were all over the East Side's mobbed, dirty streets. The city was changing uptown, where the Victorian

47

HARRY ROSKOLENKO

Age's architecture began to give away to the needs of the twentieth century. But, where I lived, in the helter-skelter of tenements, pushcarts, and gas-lit corners, everything was as it had been built. The tenements were made of bricks, wooden stairs, wooden floors, wooden doors—and great fires were as common as the cold. For heat, most people burned coal.

Great fires used to rage through the tenements during the long winters. The burned bodies would be laid out in the streets, covered with sacking or tarpaulins by the smoke-choked, ice-laden firemen hosing down the fire. They were our heroes in their peaked red fire hats. We watched them, awed by the flames burning up house after house; burning up men, women, children—and the boarders.

The wildest, saddest men among us were the boarders—often dead a year after their arrival. They were killed by accidents on the job or through falling down an elevator shaft. They died anonymously. They died with their *shifskart* money all saved up. They were tragic men in a hundred terrible ways. They worked all the time, including Sundays, which was normal in those days. They had the holy Sabbath—and after that, it was an unholy rush in every direction to make the *shifskart gelt* grow into enough for the last visit to the shipping agency that issued the ticket. It was pain and panic daily, and sadder around the holidays, when the boarder's empty life became all the more unbearable, deadly, and hallucinatory.

There was one suicide that I remember. The man lived alone in a back-house flat. He was the loneliest of them all—no longer a boarder. He had finally saved enough to get the three-room flat, which resembled every other one up front except that the sun never reached his windows.

On Saturdays he would sit in the yard after returning from the synagogue; a thin man, almost thirty, Polish-Jewish, reading a Yiddish newspaper. He would sigh. We would stare at him. Why was a man of thirty sighing so much? There was a wife, we knew, in Lodz. One day she too would come. One day his two children would rush around the yard. Balls would be thrown.

48

A *suke*, much like my father's, would be built for *Sukkoth*, said Mr. Blum, the sigher. He had the money for the *shifskart* . . . and he was sending the money within a few days.

It was sent, but he was still very sad. Five years ago he had left his wife and children in Lodz. Letters came weekly. The children were growing up. His wife, however, was forever complaining of being lonely. She was unhappy alone, said Mr. Blum. "I am unhappy too. It is not natural to live like this, is it? She's there. I'm here . . ."

The *shifskart* came back. It was not to be used. Mrs. Blum had taken a lover. Mrs. Blum was getting a *get*—a divorce.

Mr. Blum hung himself between the kitchen and the bedroom. . . .

Other wild bodies—the sad men of the back rooms and the cot —had more promising beginnings or more tragic ends. They answered advertisements in the *Jewish Daily Forward* or *The Day*, looking for bed and board. A young woman, suddenly a widow, with one child, wanted a male boarder. The obvious was never quite stated; but there was hint enough that marriage, later, would hardly be objected to. Then the boarder could exchange his back room and cot for the bedroom and a wife. Then, too, her child, aged five, a boy called Yosel, would soon be calling Sam, the boarder, "Papa."

Sam, whom I was to meet, worked as a waiter on Delancey Street, which immediately had him suspect as a marriageable man. His peripatetic trade made him accessible to all sorts of loving and fawning, married and unmarried, women. It offered him a school in erotic dramas, and psychological adventuring— obviously abnormal to the Yiddish spirit on Delancey Street. But Sam, too long alone in a cheap hotel, wanted familial surroundings. He wanted a ready-made family; a woman endlessly devoted to washing his shirts and pressing his waiter's suit.

"To be a whole *mentsch* is like having two chickens in your chicken soup," he would tell my father. "So where do I start?"

"Begin studying the newspapers—the advertisements," said my mother.

HARRY ROSKOLENKO

Sam started with *The Forward*. It contained ads for everything. Within a week Sam found what he wanted—a young woman, Leah, of twenty-eight, with a child of five. Her husband had been dead for two years. A fire in a factory had killed her husband. And now, after two meetings with Sam and ten glasses of tea, the young woman agreed to take Sam in as a boarder. Over the tea she had studied him—not as a boarder, but as a possible husband . . . and for three dollars a week, with washing but without food, Sam became her boarder in the back room.

When Sam took Yosel for walks, Sam, always the comedian, showed Yosel how fat people ate soup, sipped tea, gobbled bread, smacked their lips, wiped their chins; and how skinny people, much more patient, ate slowly—as if they hated the *lokshn* soup. He made distinctions between the poor and the rich— as eaters. Sam also whistled and danced for Yosel. He did a hora, a kazatzka, and a two-step—like a trouper at a Romanian café.

Leah was happy. She envisaged, before the end of the year, another wedding. Sam was dedicated. Sam was a warm man. Sam loved Yosel. Sam had bought another suit. His clothes were immaculate—both suits. The back room was on its way, with its boarder, to the mistress of the bedroom . . .

One Saturday Leah announced that she was going to Coney Island with Yosel to visit a relative for the weekend. They would return late on Sunday. "So sleep as long as you want, Sam," she said. "I know that on Saturday night you work very hard— for the *shlepers*. There is lox, cream cheese, corn bread, milk in the fire-escape box. *Es*, Sam. Sleep, Sam. Be well, Sam. Good-bye, Sam . . ." and she took off with Yosel.

"Good-bye, Sam," said Yosel, hugging his father-to-be.

"Good-bye, Yosela, my child," said Sam affectionately.

Twenty-four hours later they were back. The apartment looked dark. The blinds in the living room were down. Leah's bedroom, which followed the living room, looked even darker.

Leah smelled tobacco. She smelled whiskey. She sniffed . . . then rushed into the darkened bedroom.

It was *gevalt*. The huge bed that Yosel often slept in, with

50

THE TIME THAT WAS THEN

Leah, had two others—Sam, and a woman. They were closely entwined. A whiskey bottle, with the cork half out, was on the table along with hairpins, a large bra, a corset . . .

A broom was soon flaying at the bed. Two naked bodies were suddenly upright. The broom in Leah's hands kept at it—and the naked bodies were rushing about for clothes. The woman, very fat, was trying to get into her corset, Sam into his pants. It was broom, corset, pants, shoes, shirt, waist, stockings—and a shrieking Leah. . . .

Suddenly Leah opened a window—and out went anything strange. The woman's winter coat was in the gutter, followed by Sam's hat. Then his tie. Then the woman's pocketbook and whatever else was left. After that Leah went into the kitchen for the knife she used on Friday's fish—and there was blood, Sam's, running down to the floor. One swish and she had nicked Sam's wrist. Another swish and Leah wrecked the blue-green chandelier. A third swish and Yosel was crying, having ducked in time under the bed . . . and now the neighbors came running.

The neighbors demonstrated all the nuances of love, faith, and hope, in Yiddish. They tried, while demonstrating, to take Leah's knife. They kicked at Sam while grabbing for the knife. They slapped the woman and called her a *kurva*—a whore. Then they pushed both transgressors out, into the hands of a cop, Irish—who had not yet learned Yiddish on his beat. When the cop saw the knife and the blood, he called out, "If you don't drop that knife, lady, I will have to shoot at you a little bit . . ."

"A little bit," went one neighbor, "is enough, Leah. Leah, give away that knife. *Shnel!*"

And there was Leah, yelling to God, but without the knife. And there was Leah, next week, putting another ad for a boarder in *The Forward.*

Chapter 3
The Factory in My Father's Time

According to James Huneker's *New Cosmopolis*, New York, after the turn of the century, represented a vast caldron where "every race bubbles and boils and fuses" in "the dear old dirty, often disreputable, though never dull East Side." Or as Israel Zangwill expressed it, America was "the great Melting Pot where all the races of Europe are melting and re-forming" into fifty groups with their fifty languages and histories, their fifty blood hatreds and rivalries, and where "God is making the new American."

But it was not God alone who was making the new American into his own image. It was industries and the factories located on the West Side and the East Side—all over agglutinated Manhattan with its conglomerations of enterprise and energy, with its mass of people, burgeoning with sudden gifts of electricity, gas, and steam, which they had not known in the candle-lit-power days in the ghettos of Eastern Europe. God was there in every religious conceit they had; but the new God they faced was the owner, the proprietor, the boss, the *gontser macher* who employed them—and not for Christian or Judaic ethical concerns. They were there to sweat. . . .

HARRY ROSKOLENKO

I saw my first factory when I was five years old. I came as a visitor bringing a letter and an apple to my father—a letter that looked important, from a relative in the Ukraine; it had taken weeks to reach our home on Cherry Street. My mother, who had a natural sense of calamity, wanted the letter opened and read at once. But my father was at the factory and she could not read in any language. It was written in Russian . . . and when I arrived at the factory there he was, my father, soaking wet with sweat.

It was just an ordinary shop, I discovered, with nothing special about the men, the work, the heat, the dirt, the pay, the boss, the production. It was a factory with a hundred workers stripped down to their pants. All sorts of tailoring, cutting, and pressing machines were whirling, whirring and steaming away. I was fascinated for a few minutes—then I saw my father. I lost the magic of a new place at once. The inventions were gone—and there was a man of fifty, pressing a cloak with a ten-pound steam iron.

It was summer sweat, winter sweat, all sorts of sweat; bitter, sour, stinking, moldy—through all the seasons of the year. Not one fan to blow up some wind. The fans were in the boss's office. Nor were there radios, then, to make things more rhythmical, happier, more energizing. Somebody hummed or whistled. A few pigeons would reach the fire escapes for the bits of stale bread that a worker had put there—for a moment of flight and magic. The pigeons would make off, when the steam blew their way. Instead of fans there were foremen walking about, fuming and blowing, their voices like dogs barking at other dogs.

The workers seldom paused, no matter what they were at. They talked every language but English; and the foreman, when queried over some confusion in the work, answered in every language. When the foreman laughed, everybody laughed— machinelike, blending with the pigeons, the smells, and the steam, into one great bubble of gas. After the laugh—back; the moment gone, allowed, created by some eccentricity on the part of the foreman. It had likely cost the whole factory a dollar in produc-

54

tion. And no one smoked except during lunch or when a worker went to the toilet. They were watched there as well. How long does it take to urinate? I heard the foreman say in Yiddish, *"Vi lang nemt es tsu oyspishn? Or tsu kakn? Shnel! Shnel!* Hurry. Hurry—get back to work, *pisher!"*

Yes, how long to urinate, how long to move your bowels? Nothing in nature took very long over piecework or the need to produce downtown what was needed uptown at the end of the day or that afternoon. Nothing but what went on at the tables . . . and to describe the factory, from my then younger eyes, I would need more than the five senses we've been given. I would need five more, and Dante, and metaphysics; or the chemistry of the poet, with some American assistance to blueprint the factory. It was not Dante's inferno . . . for none of the workers had committed more than normal sins—like making a living, being with God, consumed about their wives and children, living in rat warrens. The factory, however, had its spiritual ingredients, for without God, or whatever the workers thought about God in their orthodox ways, life would not have been possible on any terms.

They were producing winter wear, heavy coats and cloaks, in the summertime. Outside, the temperature was almost 100 degrees. Indoors, it rose to 110 or 120—humid, steamy, all-encasing, gluey. At the tables they got so much per garment pressed or so much for sewing on sleeves, collars, linings, bodies—whatever went to make up the finished garment. It was so little usually and the cause of many strikes and sudden stoppages. With this system of sweating, every worker gave up his lunchtime—the minutes saved, to earn a bit more. Eat faster or eat less. Or eat what took up no time at all—and then back to the steam and the machines, and to the *gontser macher* barking to his dogs.

The day began in the dark, too early for the sun's rising, and it ended in the dark, too late for sun's setting. It was twelve hours, fourteen hours, sixteen, depending on what the worker needed at home. The nature of piecework had its own dictation, or strength, or fears, or all sorts of public and private mathematics and shorthand—to dictate the hours. Yes, what was needed at home? What was not? Who was coming over from Poland, Russia, Hungary—another relative? How much did the *shifskart* cost? And the money might or might not be paid back. Another pogrom, too . . . and my father had read the letter. It was a simple appeal—*Save Me* . . . and more hours were put in that week, that month . . . hours beyond reckoning. It was a death-ridden loft making a young man middle-aged and the middle-aged ancient. The skin changed daily, the lungs hourly, and the feet every second. It was the way of the factory when I was a boy. . . .

I would see my father rise at five in the morning. He had been a farmer and rising early was natural enough in the Ukraine. He would dress quietly. The children must not be disturbed because of school, because of their studies, because of our future. We might, one day, be richer than my father if we were prepared properly, he said to us. My mother was heating milk, chickoried coffee, oatmeal—breakfast. Into the coffee went brown sugar. Into the coffee went some cognac—to warm him up. The house was cold; or, when the huge stove was going, like a Turkish bath . . . and we lived between these extremes of cold and heat. And she was packing his lunch—last night's dinner.

My father was off in a hurry. On the way he picked up a Yiddish newspaper, usually the Socialist *Forward*. Since there were several ways of getting to the factory, he tried them all—for speed. He would usually take the Madison Street horsecar toward the Bowery and then walk up to Greene Street, looking at his newspaper. Or he would walk to Delancey Street for another horsecar; or, if he felt that the only air he might get that day would help him, he would walk all the way—very fast—coughing over his homemade cigarettes like an old man with TB, thinking that he was young enough for his lungs to last forever.

Once at 110 Greene Street he was in the middle of a mad mob of workers, all trying for the freight elevator. Fire buckets laced the inside of the entrance along with buckets of sand. The factory floors were wooden like the broken stairs. But the freight elevators were for freight, not for the workers—for great bundles of cloaks, bolts of cloth, linings, the guts of the factory. Porters, truckmen, horses, errand boys, and the men of the machines, all were trying to merge their way into the cable-pulled elevator, which had a safety door that slid down when the elevator slid up. But soon the men like my father gave up and were walking up the nine floors, spitting, coughing, cursing, making jokes that no one laughed at—with nine floors upward to go.

The day began in the toilet, where they stripped jackets, shirts, ties—though few wore them—and undershirts. They wore hats —for religious reasons. Each man left everything but his pants and his shoes in a green locker and locked it with his own lock. Money, a watch that cost less than a dollar, went into a pants pocket. They trusted nobody and everybody. A red handkerchief or two were taken along for sweat rags—and out they rushed to the water taps with tin quart containers for their drinking water. Now they were at their machines and pressing tables. They looked even stranger in the dark, with the dangling bulbs lighting up their small places near hell—a gang of prisoners about to break rock. It was, each man soon discovered as he set his watch, 6:00 A.M. The piecework day had begun.

Now my father was at the pressing table, a big rack to his left, with the unpressed cloaks, and one to the right, where the pressed cloaks went—and the rack to the right was the one that counted at the end of the day. So much for so much—the amount I no longer recall. The foreman counted the rack up at noon or at odd hours, when shipments were being readied. My father noted everything down in a little book that he scrawled into during the day; the amount pressed, when pressed, and the name of the boy who took them off the rack. For there was always disagreement regarding the tallies, or the truth, or the lies; and the little pencil my father wetted on his tongue to make the color come out blue was his truth. When they argued, as each man did with his foreman, there was only one truth left—each man's book in his pocket. Often, too, the foreman and the boy were working it out together—a small racket that made one old man somewhat poorer at the end of the week.

My father was, soon enough, a steam engine with his pressing iron. Here, there, top, bottom, lapels, sleeves, back—the coat was pressed, hung, noted—and he reached for another. His small body was like a piece of sculpture caught in some form of motion; an engine puffing; an engine riding into a station; a bursting continuity of steam, thin muscles, sharp reflexes—and cloak went after cloak, done, counted. On and on it went, wearing him to death.

The pressing iron had a springlike attachment overhead enabling the presser to make agile movements with it. It sprang, whirling like a symbol of everything that had gone before in the world—to make men and women look sartorial, gentle, cultured, and hardly part of the new century's mockeries about man, especially the workingman. It came like the diesel and the locomotive as some abrupt, ugly, mean machine that took you from one place to another. It said STEAM in the way it was built. It hissed the same way. It came out of men's mouths as they leaned over the work tables to make the irons move faster. They coughed, stared, pressed away—reminding me of the poem ''The Song of the Shirt.'' But it was not a shirt they were working on; these were cloaks, expensive, often with bits of fur. It was not a song either. These were not men on the Volga, though some had come from that region. They were men from a newer Manhattan, not Whitman's Manhatta; they were nine flights up on Greene Street, and the country was the United States of America.

Like the tenements we lived in, these lofts were created for massing people, boxing them in; and though the land was spacious, the working and living spaces in Manhattan were small—hardly related to the rest of what America looked like. The farmers outside of New York knew it, but not my father. As far as my father was concerned, the entire country was a loft and a factory making cloaks; for he saw nothing else. He never visited David, the farmer up at Accord, New York. To visit David would only remind him of the farm and the mill in the Ukraine . . . and he would have cried.

Of course, there were many unions in my father's time as well as the annual Labor Day parade. The celebration to honor labor was begun by an Irishman named Peter James McGuire in May 1882, through the newly created Central Labor Union of New York. Peter James McGuire, in his resolution, which bordered on Biblical rhetoric, spoke in his introduction about a day that was to go around the world and become universal—"A day to honor those who from rude nature have delved and carved all the comfort and grandeur we behold . . ." and my father had read it, years later, in Yiddish. The Jewish unions, as well as others, massed in the parades around New York, to honor, by their early radicalism, what seemed most normal to honor— their labor. What McGuire had sponsored as a workingman was made official by President Cleveland, who signed a bill on June 28, 1894, setting aside the first Monday in September as a legal holiday—without pay.

My father had his union—the International Ladies' Garment Workers' Union, begun in 1900. He was a charter member of the ILGWU, able to strike, capable of going hungry, and learning what socialism was in the course of normal events. The old century had turned—and it was now the twentieth century. America was no longer a debtor nation. It was a country of capitalism and colonialism, with the colonialism of the sweatshop adding to the overall conceits. Between 1890 and 1900 the clothing industry had more than doubled its output. From 1,224 shops in 1890 the number grew to 2,701 by 1900. The new century was banging on many doors, factories, and lofts. Capital investment in the clothing industry grew from 21 million to 48 million within ten years . . . and production went from 68 million dollars to 159 million by 1900. When my father first began on Greene Street in 1895 there had been 39,000 workers in the trade. Soon it would be 84,000, and the year was 1901.

Strikes had been very common. They were uncontrolled, private, wildcat, without a direction, though the basic impulse to organize, with a known direction and purpose, came during the general strike of 1894, a year before my father arrived. He soon learned, as did all his friends, that when his shop went on strike the struck manufacturer would move to Boston, Philadelphia,

59

or Baltimore—to other cities with European Jews. Even when
the union became national there were still runaway shops leaving
Greene Street during the wintry days. The pickets marched,
singing in Yiddish, shouting in Yiddish, proclaiming the merits
of their strike against their employers. Ironically, both worker
and employer were Jews. But one of them was on strike . . . and
my father could not run away to another city. He was never to
see Boston, Baltimore, or Philadelphia; just Cherry Street,
Greene Street, and First Avenue when he worked there, his
black boots stained red with the blood of slaughtered sheep.

He rode, he walked, he struck—and he went back to the shop
again. The pattern was part of the endless conversations about
conditions and wages. There were no conditions and hardly much
of a wage. He heard everything in the coughing. He saw it in
the glazed eyes, the thin bodies, and the hysterical speeches—
the compulsive arguments during the few minutes the men took
to eat lunch. To watch them swallow sandwiches and drink their
thermos of tea was to see a mad ballet dancing its last steps.
There were no spectators—only they, the participants, making so
many coordinated movements per minute.

Move this way, then that way. Pick up a cloak, spread it, press,
grab, hold, hang—then do it over again. When I saw my father
at it, I saw everything. There was a fog of steam insulating
him. It rose like a geyser and remained there, a halo over
piecework. Move here, there—one, two, three; and the movements joined in some wild arrangement, to get the cloak pressed
and hung up on the rack that counted. Cough and press—and
then do it all over again.

It was a carnival of steam. There were rubber cables and gas
lines leading from the floor to the ceiling, then to the tables.
Everything began and ended at the tables alongside the men
stripped down to their pants. The process was as human as the
elements used. The canvas was over the cloaks, the pressing irons
on the canvas pressing cloth, then the steam was over all. The
shop had a smell that was unique—part garment, steam, and
then the acid of the workers' pasty bodies, all merging into gar-

ments and flesh. The smell was acrid at all times—a perfume of
constant human sweat. It was a system of labor that was too old
yet too young. It was primitive yet it was sophisticated in the
sense that its various elements were weaving all the strands into
the twentieth century's scenario to mass-produce a new America,
with new Americans.

There were a few Greeks, some Italians—but mostly Jews.
None of them had a language with which to meet the others with
ease. They had only broken English broken into many separate
tongues, accents, and angers. There were words of fantasy acted
out with hands, fingers, and loud sounds . . . words of no meaning to anyone, just rebellious words sounding out something in
the heart and the head of a man, by instinct. And when they ate
they were separated by the smells—food from their own countries—olfactory nationalism—lox, pickles, onions, cabbage, sau-
sages, wine—for the more reckless of the Italians—when there
might be a bit of laughter. They met over the food, dining like
so many prisoners of their own needs—and they needed everything.

The worker who ate too long and too well was envied. Obviously his hands were faster, his body bigger, his health better,
and envy was easy, for it showed up at the end of the week in
the bigger pay envelope. As for the slower worker, he was busy
talking more—when the foreman was not around. He kidded,
gossiped, made socialistic comments. He sneered at the compulsive workers for their hurry to outdo yesterday's output. There
was a norm—yesterday's. There was today's—and that was tomorrow's gauge. It was, to the kidder and the kidded, too brutal
to see anything there as comic. There was the language of piecework—a language that had no grammar in this airless loft. Outside, up there, when my father looked up at the sky, he was
thinking of God.

And they all had dreams with religious intensity. Those who
believed and were not yet agnostics or atheists had nothing to
do with the nonbelievers. They had come over from Europe with
Judaism packed in their bundles and baggage; things of the

61

Book, words of great scribes, and the comments of the prophets
. . . and my father chose his friends in a trinity of his own making: God, the union, and the synagogue above all were his natural
affinities on Greene Street's circus of dread and death.

When the mad lunch was over, the mad afternoon began. Everything was explosive. The foremen were barking demands. The
clock that ran the loft and the machines was not a clock that
anybody knew. It had neither hands, pendulums, numbers, nor
springs. It was a private clock ticking away in the steam's ravaging rhythms of pennies, nickels, and dollars. So much steam to
a dime and ten times as much to a dollar—that was the clock
that my father knew. The dollar watch stuffed into his pants was
something he looked at when he got home, when he had dinner,
when he went to sleep, and when he got up. Time was the rasping foreman's voice echoing the foreman's own needs. It had
neither a moon nor a sun nor heroes. It was a loft with machines,
voices, wooden floors, buckets of sand and water, and a fire ax.
No architecture—just floor space, to contain the men and the
things there. Not a picture, not a mirror. The toilet was there
to keep the workers from using the hallways or the windows—
for the tokens of sanitation.

It was the twentieth century, though it scarcely looked like
it. Some laws had been passed, some had not. What was enforced
was what the unions enforced by strikes. Child labor was hardly
alien, nor was Greene Street exceptional in its practices. It was
just another narrow street of horses, trucks, and piles of goods
moving in and out of the huge lofts. My father had come there
one day in 1895 with a friend from his town who had brought
him along, to get him a job, to teach him his profession—cloak
pressing . . . and he was to quit one day in 1929, when he was
seventy years old, some weeks before Wall Street crashed, having been on Greene Street, with some time out, for more than
thirty years.

The factory had seen most of my father's middle and old age
. . . and there had been no other place, no vacation that he remembered though the unions eventually got that and he could
have had one. But, somehow, he never took it. What would he

have done with it? Where would he have gone? Where were the
green fields of the Ukraine? Were they in the Borscht Belt of
the Catskills? He was never to see that either. He saw the
entrails of the factory—and the synagogue. That was enough
for a man who pressed cloaks, ate steam, smelled acid—and took
home enough to say that he took care of us. . . . And I was to
remember, when my brothers became rich, he would say to one
of them, "Please, son, find a place where everything is green—
so I can live my last days there . . . please, son."

Is it a fictitious street or address—110 Greene Street? Hardly!
The summer before we entered World War One, when I was ten,
I knew too well the reality of it; for I spent it beside him—an
errand boy pushing loading carts to the elevator; then down the
elevator to the trucks, which went uptown into some commercial
anonymity.

"The Jewish needle," wrote Jacob Riis in 1890—and the
presser, as someone could have added—"made America the best-
dressed nation in the world." Between East Broadway, Greene
Street—and Broadway—the juxtapositions equaled out the sweat
in my father's time.

On Friday there was an exodus from the loft, and he left
earlier. It was time for the Sabbath and God—to press Hebrew
rituals into a few hours of Judaic commandments, to keep the
Sabbath holy. Then he forgot about the little brown envelope,
his pay—containing twelve dollars. But he was back again on
Sunday, though the sweat on Sunday had another kind of meaning, more Jewish and less Christian, he would say.

Yet the real religion was at the ten-pound pressing iron. But
how did one pray to it? What would the prayer have been? For
more steam to make more images of awe? What did the pressing
iron have to do with Moses? Where did Judaism start—with
steam? Were all his thoughts only the rituals of a factory? What
about . . . and we would hear, in semilearned comments, what
Rashi might have said about the factories. What Rashi said
meant little to me. There were no factories in the tenth century,
nor pressing irons—nor a land called the United States.

What was my father's trade called? He was, according to the

language of folklore, a "presser *by* cloaks." He was never, in Yiddish vernacular, called a "presser *of* cloaks." The *of* and the *by* were relative. It was not a scholarly profession. No degrees were given by CCNY for a *Professorship of Pressing*. Pressing had nothing to do with agriculture; though the wool would indeed have come off a sheep's back. But my father, scholarly enough when he had two drinks of cognac, or schnapps, would say, "That the trends uptown created the terrors downtown. *Azey iz es. . . .*" And if that's the way it was then God wanted it that way by design. "We are born to suffer," said my father.

"We are born to suffer more," said my mother.

I often wondered, later, whether they were secret members of the Dutch Reformed Church, they were so alike in their intensity and the hallowed language of the Old Testament.

There were bizarre relationships, at times. A presser that my father knew suddenly became a *macher*, via borrowed money. Some relatives had pooled their money and their skills, found a cheap loft—and like the pigeons on the window sills, they were thrown crumbs. They were nonunion contractors in Jersey City, flown there by a wind over the Hudson River. They managed for a season, botched up their skills and the mathematics of *macherism*, and were back on Greene Street—broke and pressing for a real *macher* four months later.

They pressed and they coughed. It was as ritualistic as praying at the synagogue. There were plagues around, plagues that affected your lungs. There were posters on the walls of the lofts, and one, in black and white, said, "A cough may lead to consumption." It told the workers to go to the closest tuberculosis clinic, to a dispensary, to a hospital, to a doctor. Fortunately none of us got tuberculosis. The disease was factory- and manmade. Dust, heat, stink, cigarettes, no air, bad food, no sun— and then the posters, the clinics, the doctors—and my father's funeral—in 1937.

Chapter 4
The Cloakmakers' Strike–1910

When it took place, I was too young to understand what was happening; but the strike was discussed at home and in the synagogue as if it was God's own work. Many years after the summer of 1910 I was to hear about its great glories for the man in the sweatshop . . . and my father would say, "It was like that . . ." and details would come forth. But he said it all in Yiddish, with his first phrase, "*Azey es geveyn* . . ."

Yes, it was like that—and the strike was to lay the basis for reforming the basic labor laws of New York State. There was union recognition, after a 1910 fashion, and arbitration laws; shorter hours, more for piecework, some sanitation, higher wages; some humanity mixing in with the sweat and pain amid the cloaks waiting to be hauled away from the massive lofts and sold uptown. There would be real mass unions instead of the few militants belonging to the ILGWU and associated unions.

My father worked near the Triangle Waist Factory, a company that was to make history one day in 1911. But it was the kind of history that nobody wanted, especially the dead 146 girls who burned up in the fire that gutted the factory.

The Triangle workers, in 1908, had been organized into an

employees' benevolent association, in lieu of the union wanted by the workers and not wanted by the owners. The first meeting to organize a Triangle union took place at 96 Clinton Street, in great secrecy, with one hundred workers attending it. But it was not a secret and many of the workers were fired for joining the new union-in-the-making. On September 27. 1909, Local 25 of the ILGWU struck the Triangle Waist Factory—almost a year after the initial meeting. The police, stationed at the entrance, were soon battling with the pickets. Other shops came out in sympathy, and before many days the situation was like an uprising. It became known as the "uprising of the 20,000"—and it ended in a general strike, which spread as far as Philadelphia.

My father had gone to the first Triangle meeting as a sympathetic unionist. When he came home, past dinnertime, my mother said to him, "What is it your business? They make waists—you press cloaks!"

"All of us make clothes, Chai-Sura. What is there to eat?"

"Borscht," went my mother. "How many were there?"

"Maybe . . .?" and he was lost in the borscht.

My sister Edna, who had the habit of clipping items from newspapers, especially from *The World*—and was studying to become a librarian—would read to my parents her clipped views from the American press. Years later I was to inherit a ton of her clippings, all neatly filed in folders marked *Strikes, Pogroms, Insurrections, Assassinations, Anarchism, Socialism, How-to-Be Successful, Marriage Hints,* etc., anything with a social concern . . . and now she was lecturing, like a senior librarian, to my parents. . . .

"No! No! It was not like that liberal newspaper," said my father, interrupting my sister. "Listen to me, *kinder* . . ." and he was relating what he had read about the strike—then, what he had heard, what he had seen . . .

One worker, when arrested, was lectured to by Magistrate Olmstead: "You are on strike against God and Nature, whose firm law is that man shall earn his bread in the sweat of his brow. You are on strike against God." George Bernard Shaw in

London, hearing of Olmstead's pronouncement, cabled back from the battlements of the Fabian Society: "Delightful. Mediaeval America always in the intimate personal confidence of the Almighty."

Philadelphia was the scene of similar battles, arrests, and lectures about God—not about wages, but eventually a settlement was reached there too.

The tragic drama of the massive deaths at the Triangle Waist Company on March 25, 1911, brought further progress. Complaints had been made to the mayor, to the inspectors, to the Fire Department, about the fire hazards there. Now Governor Dix appointed the New York State Factory Investigating Commission, which forced through, after two years of investigation, a total revolution in the laws regarding workers' protection in the factories. Many years later, when I was to visit the cemetery where my sister Esther was buried, I was to see more than seventy graves . . . the graves of the girls of that fire. There was a small marker over each grave. A marble arch at the entrance detailed the tragedy of that day in 1911.

"It was like that," said my father again. "When you were three years old, in 1910, the strike took place—the cloakmakers' strike. But I must tell you, *boychik*, that in 1893 a New York State factory inspector wrote: 'The cloak trade relies almost solely on tenement and sweatshop workers.' Wait, one day you'll come to my factory—and you'll see what I mean . . . and it was like that . . ."

In addition to the factories, there were the shops, or what passed for shops, in East Side tenements; in the front houses, in the yards, and the smaller back-yard houses. They were upstairs and downstairs; up five, six, and seven flights—in flats that looked like warehouses, hardly like places to sleep and to live. Small children, aged five, were already experts with the needle. They sewed buttons. They carried cloaks. They tied up cloaks. They threaded needles. They heard their tortured parents bemoan America's greatness. For this they had left Europe? Where was Europe? I hardly knew—for it was a word, a word like a

67

place called Russia, Poland, Hungary, Romania; places in another place . . . and the tenements had become a country.

A clipping of that period that Edna gave me had this to say: "Take the Second Avenue Elevated—and look out. Every open window in the big tenements that stand like continuous walls on each side will give you a glimpse of one of those shops as the train speeds by. Men and women bending over machines or ironing clothes at the window, most of them half naked. The road is like a big gangway to an endless work room with vast multitudes forever laboring. Morning, noon or night—it makes no difference. The scene is always the same. . . ."

Said another commentator: "Lofts over stables and similar places were also used for this purpose and little attention was given to keeping them whitewashed or free from vermin. The rooms were overcrowded, had little chance for ventilation, and were insufferably hot in the summer. In the early years, toilets were located in the back yards, and later when they were placed adjoining the workshop, they were so neglected that they were a frightful nuisance. . . ."

Where was all this taking place? Mostly in the Tenth Ward, where the newly arrived, who had praised the Statue of Liberty one morning as their ship passed it, lived. Now, all the members of the family were at work, sweating collectively for fourteen hours a day—to make, collectively, twelve dollars for that week.

It was a contest between small manufacturers, also recent arrivals, and the bigger ones—who had come earlier. Often, too, they were *landsleit*, friends, who went to the same *vereins* and synagogues—for some special ironies. Downtown the manufacturers were called moths; uptown—giants.

Downtown took in East Broadway, Division Street, Delancey Street, Hester Street, Greene Street—streets that were named for gentlemen and ladies of another time; when horses, tandems, and mud—not paving blocks—made up the riding and walking areas. Uptown, on Broadway, the giants were as simple as their methods of operation. But the moths, acting like moths, took over the farmed-out work, at lower rates. Somehow the moths and the giants coalesced into one huge ugliness—and fused their methods and factories into similar mammoth means of operation. One contracted and another subcontracted.

In between were the flies, lice, bugs—all operating *factories* in places the burgeoning union could not find. The union, literally, used trackers to find these hideaways. They were in cellars with the rats and the cats and the women and the children— manufacturing a way of life that made madness only too real between the buttons, the seams, the shoulders, the backs, the fronts, the linings—basting them in steam and sweat. ''What an inhuman zoo!'' went my father.

Between my father and my sister, I was soon a junior historian.

Women, as late as 1888, made up 45 percent of the total work force in the industry. By 1900 they had gone down to 22 percent. When the Italian immigrants arrived, they soon added 15 percent to the proletarians and the peasants working in the lofts, basements, and flats. Amid garlic and wine and Yiddish and Italian the garment industry work force became a huge sausage.

The workers, too often, bought their own machines, as well as the needles and thread. One worker competed against another; and the first man to buy a machine soon had others following his example. When a job ended in one loft or tenement, the worker was soon seen lugging his heavy machine to another loft; or if he could spare fifty cents, he hired a lugger to take his machine to another petty contractor. The sewing machine, like the pressing iron, was as much a part of the worker's body as his hands were, along with the cloaks and the suits.

''I could carry my own pressing irons—but a sewing machine? What insanity!'' said my father.

Machines, needles, thread, pressing cloths, oil, sponges—and the all-embracing smells of bodies, steam, and anger. These were the ever-present elements of the garment industry, but there was no oil to soothe away the anger—which went with the day, the minute, the hour, the year, machined in all its surfaces. Even the electric power was sold to the workers by some employers—a

69

HARRY ROSKOLENKO

contract within a contract. A worker was made to feel that he had a stake in the overall arrangement. Yet a subcontractor who had, some weeks earlier, been a worker, could make as much as $150 a week from his sudden emergence into another world. All he had to do was to find a place, pick a select group of non-bother-some workers, meet a contractor—and he was in business in a hurry. A month before, he had made less than $15 a week—for a 16-hour day and a 6-day week. A presser, like my father, could only marvel at the industry of some of his colleagues—bosses one day, contractors one hour, and back to the ranks of the prole-tariat in a matter of days, weeks, or months. A sort of mystique in economics or energy, plus the sheer rhetoric of Yiddish, en-abled a man to come up on top—for a few months, before he sank down again under the weight of his primitive operation.

Contemporary slavery. A day at work in a loft, then back home with more bundles. John Dyche, who had been born in Rus-sia, had worked in England as a socialist organizer, and became a union official in New York, had this to say to an investigating committee—and my sister read it to me: "After six or seven in the evening when people left their shops on Fifth Avenue, you could see those people carrying bundles home, and some of them had two machines. One machine they had in the factory and one machine they would have at home . . . and they would sit at home and work there, the wives and children helping on Saturdays and Sundays."

There was, so said some politicians and all the social workers, "deplorable industrial chaos" created by cutthroat methods, anarchistic economics, and too many willing immigrants. They came off the ship one day and they were in a shop the next day —totally confused. Ship to shop, needle to eyes, hands on every-thing—they were suddenly New Americans within the closed spaces of the lofts—not that they had known anything better where they had come from. They had merely traded the names of countries. They were awash, upended, and languageless—except for Russian, Polish, and Yiddish, which did not always help when they tried to talk to the man alongside them. It was

70

chaos. They saw it and felt it. And they talked about a strike a week after they had arrived at Ellis Island and been processed into the folklore of the United States of America.

"One day a *tsadek*—the next, a socialist," said my father. A *tsadek* is a righteous man, I knew.

The socialist leader Meyer London began an organization campaign at the Manhattan Lyceum in 1908—to change the abysmal economic spread between the worker and his employer. There were others, leaders of the union, men like Abraham Rosenberg, who had come to America in 1883 and was, between 1908 and 1914, the president of the union. He spoke along with London, and S. Polakoff, a tailor, who had come from Russia in 1897. And though the union was talking about a massive general strike, its treasury then was only some $70—hardly capital enough to rely on for two seconds during a strike. By November of that year, however, John Dyche, who supervised the finances of the union, had gotten together $126—and that was a strike fund to the Russian, Jewish, and Italian immigrants preparing for the general strike.

"What does that mean?" I asked my father.

"*Vos meynt dos?* What does it mean?" repeated my father. It meant a membership drive. "We went to everybody who had hands and eyes," my father said. "If he could walk or talk, he was soon a member. Litvaks, Galicians, a mixed-up lot of nothings —and that's the way it was. Everybody was a nothing. All they had was God on Saturday and the union the rest of the week. There were buttonhole-makers who would not talk to pressers. There were pressers who would not talk to basters . . . and then came some men who had a lot of *seykhl*—from the United Hebrew Trades, the Joint Board, the Cutters Local, and the Workmen's Circle—and we were soon ready."

The Joint Board, by various means, brought in 2,000 members. A real strike fund was created, with every member paying in two dollars. Meetings were held in shops, lofts, flats, cellars—to acquaint every worker with his own well-known condition. A newspaper was issued by the Joint Board—the *New Post*. The periodical *Ladies Garment Worker* also came out—in Italian, English and Yiddish. Each had but one story—the general strike.

In June 1910 the tenth convention of the union was held in Boston, with but seventy delegates present. It was a beleaguered convention, tossing in various directions. Five days after the convention began, Jessie H. Greenberger introduced a resolution for a general strike in New York City, to embrace the entire garment industry. When voted on, it was carried 55 to 0, and the day of the strike was left to the strike committee.

The Joint Board, made up of nine locals, began to prepare for the general strike. Within the locals were the following— for the historical record: my father's local, The Cloak-Pressers of Local 35; the Button Hole Makers Union, Local 64; the Shirt-Makers Union, Local 23; the Cloak and Shirt-Makers of Brownsville, Local 11; the Amalgamated Ladies Garment Cutters, Local 10; the Cloak-Makers Union, Local 1, and the Cloak and Suit Tailors, Local 9. They were the initiators for the general strike. . . .

Agitating committees were set up along with picketing committees and relief committees. It was the beginning of meetings by committees, the use of lawyers, the hiring of halls—heretofore literally unknown as sociological artifacts. The American Federation of Labor was appealed to—and organized labor not within the Federation. On June 28, 1910, a test mass meeting was held to gauge the nature of union support . . . and Madison Square Garden turned away thousands of proletarians with bizarre accents, when Samuel Gompers addressed the meeting.

More meetings. Shops, factories, cellars—wherever there were workers, they met, to vote. Those favoing the strike numbered 18,771. Those opposed—615. The date, 2:00 P.M. Thursday, July 7, 1910 . . . and the great revolt was on.

The day my father was talking about I was to read about, years later.

In his pithy book, *Memoirs of a Cloakmaker*, Abraham Rosenberg, who was one of the leaders, recalls: ''About two o'clock some of the members of the strike committee together with some

representatives of the press went to the cloak district to see how
the order of the strike committee would be taken. . . . Among
those who were curious to see whether the workers would re-
spond were A. Cahan and B. Schlesinger, editor and manager
of the *Forward*. Our people naturally were excited, their hearts
beat fast, and every minute seemed an age to them. When ten
minutes past two there was no worker to be seen, Cahan ironically asked: 'Well, where are your strikers?' . . . Hardly had he
spoken, than we saw a sea of people surging from all the side
streets towards Fifth Avenue. Every minute the crowds grew
larger, and all moved in the same direction. By half-past two, all
the streets, from Thirty-eighth Street down and from the East
River towards the west, were jammed with workers. In many
of the streets, cars and trucks had to be stopped because of the
crowds. The workers were carrying their tools and were moving
in the direction of the halls where they were to meet, according to
the instructions of the *New Post*. . . . Many of our most devoted
members cried for joy, at the idea that their lifelong labors had
at last been crowned with success. In my mind I could only picture to myself such a scene taking place when the Jews were
led out of Egypt."

Roll calls were held twice a day, for the 60,000 workers—to
see who was scabbing. The pickets, en masse, roamed from shop
to shop, to assist shops that were weakening. It was a holiday
in hell, said one observer—but the workers were doing their own
dancing there. There were almost constant arbitration and rumors. There were rumors of rumors and rumors of settlements
that were not settlements. Those who needed money to hold out
were helped—two dollars a week to the unmarried, at best, and
four to the married. "How did we live?" asked my father. "We
didn't!"

The strike committee that evenutally settled it set up head-
quarters at Twenty-third Street and Fifth Avenue, at the Vic-
toria Hotel. They had nineteen demands, including some that
seem quite simple today: a 48-hour week; the abolition of subcontracting; work equally distributed among the workers—and

no favoritism. Other demands included the employment of a shop steward, to oversee all the mathematics and the mechanisms of work and payment within the shop. And since the closed shop was one of the basic demands of the union, it was on the top of the ragged cream pie.

"The closed shop meant everything," said my father.

The manufacturers, as a protective association, took advertisements in the newspapers, picturing their workers as well paid and a most happy lot of men. Mr. M. J. Reagan, who was an arbitrator for the New York State Department of Labor, entered —to arbitrate. Arbitration was new—and confusing. "Every cloakmaker was a lawyer now," added my father. "Ar-bit-rate? *Vos far a meshugas meynt* ar-bit-rate?"

On July 17, the Manufacturers Association was supposed to meet with ten representatives of the union—but they never met. Instead there were challenges, attacks, reprisals, and fulminations on both sides, each accusing the other of trying to wreck the industry and make it nonprofitable. Within a brief time, however, the smaller manufacturers, numbering more than 300, signed up with the union and recognized most of the nineteen demands made by the union.

It was giant and moth, boss and worker. Soon various large department stores, with their stocks down, entered the negotiations —especially A. Lincoln Filene, of Boston. With him came the jurist Louis Brandeis, to argue before the strike committee about the meaning of the *closed shop*. To some, the meaning was obvious. It meant control of the shop. To others it was semantic nonsense, open to all sorts of interpretations—and Mr. Brandeis was a lawyer. Various members of the Joint Board made their own secret agreements or they attempted to do so. There was a possibility that the union would split apart, and Samuel Gompers, of the American Federation of Labor, decided to meet with all parties in a final decision-making meeting.

Mr. Louis Brandeis, later to serve on the Supreme Court, was the chairman of the meeting that evaluated the various propositions for three days. Among the twelve items discussed by the various arbitrators were the methods of enforcing conditions in

74

the shops; sanitation; wages; subcontracting; wages to be paid weekly; overtime for nightwork; who was to pay for the electricity and the materials; the tenement sweatshops, and discrimination against union workers. It was to evolve the classical formulas for later strikes and settlements.

My sister found something in one of her folders and she read aloud what had occurred on the first day of the strike: Julius H. Cohen, legal expert for the manufacturers, said: "There has never been a time when we have not admitted that there were grievances that our employees have. . . . We have gone into the conference, gentlemen, not merely for the purpose of adjusting those grievances, but for the purpose of finding out some way by which this awful waste may be avoided in the future. . . . We come in a meek and humble spirit, solely because we are realizing the big social problem we are facing at this table here."

Various points divided the union and the employers—especially the length of the working week. The employers offered their workers a 53-hour week, with a half holiday on Saturday.

My father laughed, but in a grim sort of way, then said— "The Sabbath is Sabbath—all day! How much of God would I know if I worked half of the Sabbath?"

The union insisted on a 49-hour week. The rest of their demands came in this fashion: Cutters, $26.00 a week; Jacket Pressers, $22.00; Underpressers, $18.00; Skirt Pressers, $20.00; Skirt Basters, $15.00; Skirt Finishers, $12.00; Buttonhole Makers, $1.10 per one hundred buttonholes. . . .

Both sides argued. It hung on the mathematics of the buttonhole, in the end; the minor and the major ingredients of time, plus movement, plus accomplishments. But the main issue, obviously, was the question of the closed shop. For without a closed shop what did the union gain for its members? It was to be the salient and definitive question—with judicial answers. Mr. Louis Brandeis was to come up with a solution-within-a-solution, enough to have a university named after him.

Said Mr. Brandeis about a thought that he had regarding something he called "the preferential union shop": "The unions should be so strengthened that in the course of time they might

75

have practically all, if not all, of the operatives in the shops as members.''

To the union leaders, this was a totally new idea. My sister was again at her folders. The *Jewish Daily Forward* wrote editorially, ''The preferential union shop was the open shop with honey.''

And my father chimed in, ''There was, then, not enough money in the honey.'' My sister laughed—then came more of her librarian's social data . . .

Others entered into the primitive skills of arbitration, especially the socialist leader, Meyer London, who said: ''Let us make one final effort with our joint brains. . . .'' But there was no juncture and no legal formula that could measure up to such a declaration. Everybody was too far apart on too many issues; and the complexity behind the meaning of the phrase *''the closed shop''* involved the language of action before there was a final signature to an agreement.

The manufacturers asked for an injunction. Their lawyer, Mr. Cohen, said, prior to getting the injunction: ''The manufacturers can and will declare in appropriate terms their sympathy with the union, their desire to aid and strengthen the union, and their agreement that as between union and nonunion men of equal ability to do the job, they will employ union men. The manufacturers seek the union shop, by which they mean a shop in which union standards prevail and the union man is entitled to the preference.''

A temporary injunction was granted by Justice Lehman. A leader of the pickets said the ''bosses tried to employ guards with or without badges, but our men felt that the strike was a question of life and death to them and having said their prayers, went forth to meet the guards.''

To most of New York's newspapers, the strike was to become a moral struggle. *The New York Times* was not sympathetic to the strikers, nor were most of the other newspapers. Only the socialist papers, the Yiddish *Forward,* and the English-language daily the *New York Call* came out in support of the strike. It was the beginning of the latter-day class struggle, if in strange ways.

Restaurants that had served workers prior to the strike now fed them for free. Even some bankers gave money to the strike fund. College students helped to picket shops—and many came from the fashionable schools for future ladies and gentlemen. And those workers who had already settled with their employers gave 15 percent of their earnings to the strike fund. Between July 7 and September 27, $246,000 was collected. The Yiddish newspaper, *The Forward*, collected more than $60,000 for strike benefits, for there were many hungry families on the Lower East Side. I never asked my father how he managed to feed us during those innocent dialectical days of my youth. That he managed was enough for me.

Another meeting. Another almost-acceptable agreement. But the general strike committee was divided. What does one give up—the closed shop? Now the workers themselves were divided. Weeks had passed. "There was mass hunger and not enough union funds to bake a small bread for a family," recalled my father, in some sentimental reflections about his life as a socialist who believed in God.

On August 26, more arbitrators presented new suggestions regarding the preferential shop, including a 52-hour week and the matter of pay to be arbitrated in the future. But these proposals were rejected en masse on August 27, when they were presented to the strikers at meetings throughout the city.

The police, as was their custom in those days, were intimidating the pickets. Justice Goff, of the Supreme Court of New York, finally issued an injunction making both the strike and the closed shop illegal. *The New York Times*, according to my sister, said in an editorial that it was "the strongest decision ever handed down against labor." Most of the newspapers in New York agreed and condemned Justice Goff's injunction.

There were more meetings—and, finally, on September 2, an agreement was reached.

Sixty thousand workers had been out on strike for nine weeks —and what they won was to become the standard that other unions were to use later on. They had arbitrated, talked endlessly, broken off talks—and with cigarettes, beer, whiskey, and sandwiches they had come to some conclusions about each other's value in the marketplace of the clothing industry in New York City.

The settlement, known as the Protocol for Peace, gave the strikers eleven conditions. My sister read them aloud to us from the newspaper:

10 legal holidays with full pay

A regular weekly wage and in cash

The preferential shop

Committees of sanitation in each shop

No more subcontracting

Electrical power to be charged to the employers

A 50-hour work week

Double time for overtime

New piece rates—to be established by committees

$3 more—as the minimum scale

Freedom of selection in hiring and firing

I quote again from Abraham Rosenberg's *Memoirs of a Cloak-maker*: "As soon as it became known that a settlement had been reached, thousands of workers, cloakmakers and others, began to gather in the streets leading to the Square where the Forward Building is located. By seven o'clock, the Square and the nearby streets were jammed with people. . . . The whole district was on its feet that night. The scene is indescribable! No one who has not witnessed it can ever have a clear picture of it. Everywhere men and women, old and young, embraced and congratulated one another with the victory. It was early morning, Saturday, September 3, before the streets were emptied of the masses of humanity. . . . Saturday afternoon, September 3, trucks decorated with flags, with bands of music, and carrying crowds of cloakmakers drove through the streets, announcing to all and sundry that the strike had been settled."

And my father would say when I was a boy, when we talked about the times of the strike—"*Azey es geveyn.*" Yes, it was like that in the sweat of his brow. . . .

78

Chapter 5
Portrait of a Socialist

In 1907, when I was born, there were 2,100 conservative Republicans in the Eighth Assembly District, 3,146 self-indulgent Democrats, 7 nonwayward citizens who preferred the Prohibition Party, 46 voters for the iconoclastic Socialist Labor Party, and 803 stalwart proletarians who voted for the virtuous Socialist Party. By 1912, the nimbler Democrats had gained a few votes. The greatest gainer was the Progressive Party, whose members shared a liking for woman suffrage, if not the Gibson Girls, in their "rainy-daisy" skirts trailing the gutters—and Roosevelt's Populism, an in-between socialist-capitalist idea which got Teddy Roosevelt, the all-American rugged symbol, 88 votes in the Electoral College.

From 1900 to 1912, the Socialist Party had gone from 253 votes in the Eighth Assembly District to 835—a gain of more than 300 percent in twelve years. But that was only a voting statistic, for there were more Socialists around who could not vote —without citizen papers—than could, and it was Uncle Solomon, in his shop, who was making concerned noncitizens converts to Marxism, East Side style.

Uncle Solomon was a citizen. Like my father, he had come

over from the Ukraine in 1895, some 403 years after Columbus had discovered America. He lived in the Ninth Congressional District, and he convinced—from soapbox and synagogue, from toilet to horsecar, from cafes to parks—some of the 5,969 workers who had voted there for the Socialist Party. "We are better than the Democrats. How much did they get? Just 5,000 stolen votes, or they paid each thief two dollars a head for his black soul."

Uncle Solomon's statistics were his own, somewhat bookish, and a Yiddish newspaper's facts. He got bits and pieces from his colleagues tailoring over their sewing machines and tables, for talk was an ingredient of work—certainly for Jews. Between Uncle Solomon's folkways of getting current history, and my own walks and wanderings as a Jewish newsboy, we were, collectively, litle historians of odd social data. What he did not know I told him—like the fact that the Chinese lived west of Chatham Square, the Greeks closer to us, and the Arabs, Syrians, and Turks lived on Washington Street, by the docks off West Street. Obviously, I could not sell Jewish newspapers there; but I went there to see the bigger ships, smell the all-overpowering bazaars, and think of houris. When I told Uncle Solomon that I had seen a photograph of a "houri" outside a Turkish coffee-house, he slapped my face and told my father that I was chasing *kurvas* at the age of eight.

I was chasing Jews, to buy my papers; and the Jews looked like Turks and Arabs to my eyes then. Mustaches, beards, old clothes, poor—that was enough.

"They are proletarians," said Uncle Solomon.

"What is a proletarian?" I asked.

"A man who works for wages," he said like a ball off a bat.

"Am I one?"

"No, not yet."

"Will I be one?"

"I hope not—be a teacher or a professor—anything but a worker."

"Why not?"

80

"Look at your father—he's an old man before he's forty-five."

"But you're not an old man, Uncle Solomon," I said.

"I'm only forty—young, strong, full of socialism and Judaism. I believe in God—and that's enough for any man."

"I'm only eight—and I feel only half like you. . . ."

"Good, so here's a penny and buy something big for it—like the Singer Building if not the Woolworth Building . . ."

My father, through reading all the Yiddish newspapers, especially *The Forward* and the Yiddish magazines, came across names like Karl Marx, Engels, Ferdinand Lassalle, and Eduard Bernstein—German socialists. Two were Jews. Engels had been a Protestant, and Karl Marx had been a moral mishmash—a *meshumed*, Uncle Solomon called him. He was the son of a convert—and that would send him to Gehenna, said Uncle Solomon. I shuddered. That was hell—deep down with the fires in the center of the earth. I was on top of Cherry Street, with my Jewish brethren.

Uncle Solomon and my father worked in the same sweatshop—and everybody there talked about something that was either good or bad. *Bad* was what was happening in the shop all day; *good* was what happened on Friday and Saturday at the synagogue, or at the socialist meetings that Uncle Solomon went to once a week, at times, when he allowed others to talk, even to listen. In the shop it was talk and cigarettes, both coming together. They talked of wages and the union. It was always the union—like God. It was forever the Socialist Party, then our political Messiah, to Uncle Solomon . . . and to my father, who hardly had the learning of Uncle Solomon. Whatever my father heard was eleventh-hand.

All sorts of names were shouted out at the shop—and then some quaint facts, all of which came to me as a twelfth retelling, by my father. He had heard, one afternoon, about a group called the Utopians. He got all the names wrong—from Robert Owen to Sir Thomas More to Charles Fourier—which Uncle Solomon, when he came on Saturdays after the morning service at the synagogue, to have the big Saturday *tsholnt* with us, soon corrected. He would, for my stumbling benefit, spell out the names correctly. He told us about the split in the Russian Social-Democratic Party—whatever that meant to me then.

What was a split? I did that on roller skates. I also did the spreadeagle, I said, showing off my skating scholarship.

That got me two sneers, a small *potsh*—a slap—a few rebukes and we were back to a man named Lenin, who had a small beard like my father; then another man named Trotsky, who also had a small beard. They had split, said Uncle Solomon, now the theoretician of splits, Russian beards, Germans with larger beards—and all sorts of foreigners who were also bald-headed—and splitting.

Having eaten the main dish, the *tsholnt*, having drunk a few glasses of schnapps, and gone on to the compote, cakes, and tea —Uncle Solomon now theorized like a bearded conglomeration of Russians and Germans. He had a head full of socialist theories, all meaning almost nothing to me; but my father was nodding agreement, my brothers were sleeping, my sisters were clearing away the dishes, my mother was organizing my sisters—and Uncle Solomon on the sofa was challenging the capitalistic world in our tight little living room. When Uncle Solomon went back to utopianism, I challenged him, saying, "But we are utopians down in the street all the time. When we play marbles, punchball or handball, or chase the Irish, it is give-and-take utopianism, Uncle Solomon."

Uncle Solomon, vexed, retorted, "Who gives and who takes? What has a game of handball or a street fight to do with utopianism?"

I answered gamely: "I punch the ball against the wall. It comes back and my friend punches the ball against the wall. . . ." I had heard him say, once, something about mutual aid—and now I used that phrase: "That's mutual aid, punching the ball up and back, Uncle. Somebody wins. Somebody loses. Sometimes we break even—so that's socialism and utopianism and splits, yes?"

My sisters laughed from the kitchen. I laughed back from the living room. My brothers snored between everything—and my father said sarcastically, "He's a socialist leader outside the stable, where they play with that stupid rubber ball. Sell more papers! Then you can buy your own shoes. . . .''

I was most quiet, expecting another smack; but Uncle Solomon patted me, kissed me, then told me the names of a few books to read. What I did not understand I was to write down and to ask questions next Saturday. I agreed, humbled by my sudden intrusions into the adult world, hoping to fall asleep from the heavy meal and escape the wrath of my father for my awkward analogies.

The Lower East Side was a small nation unto itself, holding within its tenements and colorful streets half the Jewish immigrants in the United States. When you left its overwhelming environs, you ran into some bellicose Irish, a few mustached *shikered* Poles, some fighting, bellowing Russians—all coming out of different cellar saloons. A form of anti-Semitism was always a block away, in some cellar, falling up from a cellar, with the word Yid or Zhid, soon on your ears—and you were running for a block. Many Poles and Russians also lived within our midst, but they were the peaceful, warm, friendly Russians and Poles who sat with our mothers, wrapped in shawls, talking Russian and Polish about the Old World. It was not about socialism, but about streams, flowers, old songs, snow, gardens, children—peasant things. At school, at P.S. 31, on Monroe Street, many of the children of these Poles, Russians, and Irish were my friends— but they never talked about socialism either. It seemed to be a specially Jewish subject, and taboo. It was as tough to be a socialist as it was to be a Jew; and both, in their separate ways, became something compelling to me as words that caused people, or strangers, or friends, to brawl. There were German socialists, I heard, up in Yorkville, which made us political equals, but they were not Jewish. It was painful and puzzling in too many ways, with Uncle Solomon preaching away like an Old Testament prophet, if over compote, tea, and schnapps.

Who was not a socialist in those days? We didn't control the

HARRY ROSKOLENKO

Lower East Side of New York, but the Socialist Party membership, in 1912, rose to 125,826 stalwarts. The party had elected 160 councilmen, 145 aldermen and 56 mayors in the country. The total vote, for Debs, was 897,000—for the presidency.

In 1912 the Socialist Party had grown massively. By 1914 party membership decreased to 118,000—but it still included Uncle Solomon. There were socialists like Sherwood Anderson, Charles A. Beard, George Bellows, Floyd Dell, John Dewey— and me, going from age six to seven, eight, nine, and ten. I was freewheeling in my head about things that would make men equal, with Uncle Solomon, the theorist and activist, telling me about the Utopia that was about to arrive—just before I became twenty-one years of age and therefore able to vote for socialism.

There was, said Uncle Solomon, William Haywood, the leader of the IWW, who had broken away from the Socialist Party. He believed in sabotage and direct action—something we did all the time in the streets when we fought against the Irish and the Poles . . . and Uncle Solomon, a man of many texts, pockets, quotes, and with a great memory, would quote from the Socialist Party position: ''The use of sabotage or violence made for guerrilla warfare, demoralized those who employed these methods, and opened the door to the agent provocateur.'' It was a lesson by rote, drilled into my questing head much as if I should not pat a dog that most certainly had rabies. And so I asked, then age nine, ''What is an agent provocateur?'' The word ''provocateur'' came out with many alien sounds and was blurred on my tongue.

''An agent provocateur,'' said Uncle Solomon sagely, ''is a man, a spy, hired by the police or the government to create a state of mind among workers that will make them use sabotage and direct action. Bombs, fire—anything. Do you understand that, Harry?''

I said, ''Of course! Of course! Of course, Uncle Solomon. I understand.''

I understood nothing at all about agents and their provocateurs. He explained it again, giving me more examples about bombs and fires. There were famous agent provocateurs. He

84

named many Russians and I instantly forgot the names. Now I know them.

My father served more tea and schnapps. It was our Saturday afternoon lecture in a half-sleepy household. We had done all things that were right—for God; now we were talking about man, on the Sabbath. And Uncle Solomon was saying, "In Russia or in Switzerland or in Paris there is a man named Lenin. He is a Bolshevik. He writes against us—as socialists. He writes against anarchists who believe in direct action. He writes about the seizure of power by the working class. Do you understand what I mean?"

I did not, of course. Seize power? What a phrase that was! Grab, take, run. Those words had been used in my English class. But "power"—that was like gas, electricity, horses and electric automobiles. I was confused by words. Many words actually took on different meanings. In my early years I said one thing when I really meant something else. There was the word "svelte," for instance. I took that to mean *zaftik*—juicy, or luscious. But "seize power," with Uncle Solomon's grave intellectuality, made me, at age nine, hardly ready to lead the working class or my handball-playing friends from the stable walls against City Hall. There, Uncle Solomon said, all the power lay in New York City —with Mayor Gaynor.

I went back to that Russian, Lenin. I asked with dutiful design, "Uncle Solomon, has Lenin written anything bad against you?"

My father laughed. Uncle Solomon laughed—and everybody not asleep laughed as Uncle Solomon, trying to follow my wayward mind, answered, "Not yet, *boychik*. But if I become a leader like Morris Hillquit, then Lenin will denounce me for believing that we can legislate our way peacefully toward socialism."

"What does legislate mean?" I asked, a word I should have known from my class in civics.

He answered, touching his little beard, sipping tea, taking another hurried drink of schnapps, saying, "It means that you educate all the people to vote the way you think—to vote for

85

socialism. That you do not throw bombs; that you do not kill presidents, mayors, governors, congressmen, the Irish, the Jews, the Polish, the Russians, the Germans; that you do not kill anybody. You vote, you understand, *boychik*?''

"And how long will that take? Maybe by next November?''

"Not by next November. Many years away in November, *boychik*. After all, all we have is some thousands of members of the Socialist Party in the United States. When we have about a million then we will have some real political power. . . .''

"And how many members does the Democratic Party have and the Republicans and the Progressives and the DeLeonites, whom you don't like? How many, Uncle Solomon?''

What a midget theoretician I was about to become!

"Who knows? They don't give out the numbers; but between the Democrats and the Republicans, they own the country. Mayors, governors, congressmen, assemblymen, the police, the firemen, the dogcatchers, the teachers—and who knows what not? It starts from the top and it goes down to the bottom. At the bottom they are in the saloons. At the top they are on the top. Do you understand from the top to the bottom?''

That was easy enough. Top, bottom, center—and off on the sides. It was the same with our gang fights. Those on the bottom of the pile were getting their noses and backs broken; those on the top were doing the breaking. Uncle Solomon was a professor of many things, my father assured me as I reached for the schnapps and had my hand slapped.

But Uncle Solomon did not have a wife. He had friends—girls and women who worked in the shop or whom he had met at the various meetings he was forever attending. Occasionally he would bring one woman over. She was stout, about thirty-two, had large breasts, wore a dangling watch over her bosom, had rosy cheeks, talked Russian, had her hair bundled back. Rachel had all sorts of complaints. Never about her health, of course. She looked as if she could pick up with ease the 50-pound piece of ice that my father lugged up the stairs for the icebox. But she complained about an old complaint—she wanted to get married to Uncle Solomon, then forty. She said to my mother, in Russian and in Yiddish, that while Uncle Solomon might be a very good socialist, he would never make a good husband.

"After forty, what can you do with a man? Make him sit down in a chair when he wants to walk, stand, run, jump, and shout? Make him drink tea when he wants schnapps? What can you do, Chai-Sura?"

"Nothing with nothing. Find another man. And while you are finding one, find a *gevir*, a richer one. For instance, there is that tailor who owns his own shop on Madison Street. His wife died two years ago. Of course, he's not so *frum*—and that's bad. He never goes to the synagogue. He's not a socialist. He's just busy fixing vests, pants, and jackets. He's also got three children; so you won't have to get pregnant. Enough is enough. How big a family do you want? He's clean, too. He has no beard. Do you want to meet him?"

Uncle Solomon laughed and had another schnapps. My father grinned. It was all old talk—whenever Rachel came. My mother always had some tailor or a small grocer—all suddenly without wives and with rooms filled with children.

"I will leave the shop," said Rachel, "and Solomon's branch of the Socialist Party. I won't see Solomon anymore by next week. . . ." And then the beginning of another tear, a handkerchief, my mother soothing her, my father embarrassed, Solomon amused at the tragicomic nuances, and again hearing what he had heard for several years, from Rachel—"And then you won't see me anymore, Solomon. . . ." The handkerchief was once again wiping away some external pain, and then the final words, "I am thirty-two, Solomon. How long can a woman wait?"

"Yes, how long?" went my mother.

"Who asked you?" asked my father.

"Rachel! God! Everybody!"

"What shall I do?" went Rachel again.

"I know what I will do," said Solomon. "I'll find someone else to cook a few meals for me, Rachel. You are not the only

87

sheyne one. Beautiful women are everywhere. So some are not socialists. So I might find just anybody. Perhaps an anarchist?"

"Not an anarchist!" said Rachel in shock. "At least a Zionist, Solomon. Please!"

"So a Zionist, all right. A little fatter, perhaps. Someone bigger, happier, a *baleboosteh.* . . ."

"Like Rachel, perhaps?" asked my mother.

"Like Rachel?" went my father.

"Like Rachel?" I was saying along with the rest.

"Who is not so fat," said my mother. "Let it be Rachel then, Solomon."

"Let it be Rachel then," said Solomon, tired, resigned, finished with the weekly battles; his private life and his public life as a socialist all mixed up.

Where would it end, he wanted to know. "Children, *kinder*— a bedroom full? Enough—so we'll get married, Rachel. Imagine marrying an anarchist? Or a Democrat? A socialist, yes . . . so no more handkerchiefs, Rachel. And where shall we move? You have one room as a boarder and I have another room as a boarder, which is not very good. Yes, a place like this—all the rooms running together; socialist rooms with equal space; a stove in the kitchen; a washtub that is also the bathtub. A line in the yard for hanging up the washing. Diapers, noise, roaches— what not, Rachel. A real home. *nokh.* . . ." And everybody was kissing everybody.

I got kissed by Rachel. I had said the last "like Rachel" to convince Uncle Solomon that even socialists had to marry more than their texts. Rachel was taking her watch off her large bosom and pinning it on my mother's bosom; a gift, a token, a piece of time that ticked over the heart and told everybody what the human time was.

In two months Solomon married Rachel. In three months both of them dropped out of the Socialist Party, saying, whenever they called on us, "There are so many things to do around the house. Soon there will be *kinder* . . . and I must take an extra job," added Solomon. "When can I go to a meeting? Look how fat Rachel is now. Socialism is for the young, *boychik*. I am too old to fight—or too much married already. . . .'' Whatever the reasons, Uncle Solomon found them at will.

In a few years he was to open his own tailoring store, hire one man, become the smallest of the smallest employers—and start contesting about value, price, and profit with his one employee. But both voted socialist in that little store on Montgomery Street, off East Broadway, opposite the yeshiva.

And this was Uncle Solomon, who had brought socialism to our house; all the mixed-up data and some of the European names that later went into history; all the illusions and tragedies; and to me, quite directly, all the years that I was, later on, to give over to another variation of Marxism—direct-action style. I'd had the peaceful lectures and Uncle Solomon's idealism; then memories and mementoes that did not stay too well, as a method. For between 1928 and 1938 I was to live the life of a Trotskyite activist; without bombs but with some theories about *permanent revolution*.

When Uncle Solomon died in his tailor shop, he no longer had an employee. He had worked alone in his last years. His family? Two sons; one became a lawyer, another a doctor. That's the way it went in the next generation down on the Lower East Side. They became Liberals, Democrats, Republicans—and they remembered some few things about the men of their father's time. Their time was hardly the factory, or socialism, or *tsholnt*, schnapps—and the talk of those days, when I was a boy.

Chapter 6

Bargains in Everything–
Orchard Street

They streamed to New York's Lower East Side during the 1880s—an eruption of Jewish migrants from Russia, Poland, and Eastern Europe, all seeking the *Goldeneh Medina*—the blessings of Mecca, American-made, in the tenements suddenly being built and the first ghettos created in the United States.

What narrow streets the ghetto streets were! What are the names or what were their names then? I am going back, at the age of sixty-three, to the streets named after many English counties and some of England's past nobility, like Essex and Suffolk. The names are still on the lampposts in 1971—to haunt the newer citizens in the packaged municipal buildings that have replaced, with some taller ugliness, the short, squat tenements that I knew as a child. Though most of the tenements have gone or are going, the people who first lived in them went long ago; and so did their children and their children's children—to Long Island, Westchester, Florida, California, Israel. The people of this area have been in transition since the 1920s. My parents, too, moved away from the bargains, the streets, the Lower East Side —to try for other bargains on other streets of New York City.

HARRY ROSKOLENKO

When we lived on Cherry Street, Orchard Street had seen better days. Once part of the vast Delancey farm of colonial times, it had been laid out as a private thoroughfare prior to 1767. James Delancey was a Loyalist, however, and after the Revolution his lands were confiscated and sold in parcels—for a total of $234,198.75—by the Commissioners of New York. Officially opened in 1806, Orchard Street—so named because it ran through the old Delancey orchard—became a favorite drive for the people of the area, especially in the springtime when the fruit trees were in bloom.

In my time it was a conglomerate street; a street that Jews and other Europeans would come to know very well. The same sort of bargaining took place all along the seven blocks of stores and pushcarts that made up the length of Orchard Street. The seven-block area began at Houston Street and ended at Division Street—a half mile of gilt, garbage, finery, and fantasy. It was a nightmare of blocks and values in everything. It was, too, a street of horses and wagons, and men carrying great loads on their backs. The men humped the enormous caravans of goods, furniture, barrels of herring—like so many camels walking through the massive congestion. The signs on the stores were mostly in Hebrew or Yiddish, with some occasional English lettering to help out the strangers from uptown or the Gentiles wandering about Orchard Street's bargains.

But the signs were hardly essential. The smells told you everything in one burst; for everything in the stores and on the loaded pushcarts was up for hurried sales. An entire pushcart's cargo of secondhand goods went in one day, because there were few places to store the unsold goods. It went to the many buyers fiddling with money, bargaining over prices, reluctant to say *yes*, constantly saying *no*; though both buyer and seller were endlessly aware that both goods and money would, soon enough, change hands.

The working and shrieking personnel were couples, their children, and their relatives. If they owned a store, the family lived in the back and worked in the front. Their day began when

92

the sun rose. It ended when the door closed—late at night. It was a timeless world that operated according to no known human schedule. The only schedule was money—and that had no clock at all. It was a blueprint in the head, hands, stomach, and ears. It made them harum-scarum and beleaguered, yet disciplined by the bizarre designs of their past in Europe. There the making of money had been much harder. In New York the *Goldeneh Medina* was a pushcart or a store on Orchard Street.

The stores had a relative function, for whatever you bought in a store cost more. It was better, less secondhand, more akin to a place called *uptown*. The flamboyant displays in the streets, however, were the lure that brought hordes from the Bronx and Brooklyn to the bargains that were the first, the last, and the best in the United States of America—or so they were constantly told in Yiddish by the first barkers in America. The pushcart market had a kind of universal economics—cheap. Everything in the cosmos was on a pushcart for somebody at some sort of price. The bakeries, with their pushcart adjuncts, sold the various breads of the world. Russian, Polish, Hungarian, Austrian, German—all heavy, all good, all the breads with or without every variation of *kiml*, or caraway seed, were there. None of the breads had paper wrappings because nothing came that way then; and one had to touch and smell the bread before it was shoved into the great shopping bags that all mothers carried when they went to Orchard Street's universal market.

The pushcarts came small, came large, came bigger than large —and in double or triple tiers. If they sold fruit—and the fruit often came from the Middle East as well as the United States— it would be piled high on double-tiered pushcarts. If it was piled with extreme care, in some sort of cubistic arrangement, the price was assuredly higher. If the fruit was just a mass and a tumble, the price was lower. Then you examined it. You picked and chose. You listened to the owner say things that were not exactly the nicest words in Yiddish. You were a *shnorer*, a beggar, obviously. "So hurry up and *shnor* at another pushcart."

The horses, too, especially in the summer, were as interesting

as the people. The horses wore straw hats. Occasionally they had
flowers over their necks, or bells, to charm the children and
make the mothers stop—by demand. They were fed oats. They
were watered at corner troughs or by pails, and when the horses
were about to create some future fertilizer the peddler would
start a Yiddish harangue that must have baffled the poor beast,
who, by now, was getting all the Yiddish accents it had ever
heard messed up in the cursing. But despite their contribution to
our local agriculture we loved the horses and their costumes. We
patted them while being warned about being bitten, and we gave
them our stolen lollipops for a quick lick before finishing them
ourselves.

To buy a suit on Orchard Street was something of a Yiddish
drama done in mock tragedy. It was inventive, if without a
known script—commedia dell'arte, totally. When I was five years
old I had my basic introduction to that bit of theater, Yiddish
fashion. It was my first suit, Orchard Street Style. I learned a
unique sort of Marxist dialectics that afternoon in value, without
any real price, and some strange sort of profit. Whatever took
place that Sunday afternoon became memorable to me for many
reasons, because it had a myth within its circumlocutions and
drama—the *landsman* myth.

My father took me to a store a little below Orchard Street. The
store was on Division Street, just where Orchard Street ended
its bargains and the new ones began on Division Street. A *landsman* owned the store. He had a name, of course. My father and
the Division Street *landsman* greeted each other as if they had
not seen each other since 1895; it was, I recall, 1912 when the
suit was being bought.

The visit looked like a perfectly normal one. Hands shook
hands. Words passed words—Yiddish, Russian, and Polish words
of a gentle nature. There was social chitchat, as well as religious
moments of concern for the soul—the *neshuma*. There was politics—mostly socialistic, but politics; and thoughts about somebody's relatives sick with cancer, then a new disease to us, and
most frightening when we learned just what it did.

My father was dealing with somebody from his own *shtetl*—

94

Above
Immigrants arriving
in New York Harbor in
the early 1900s.

Below
Immigrants arrive at
Ellis Island in 1890.

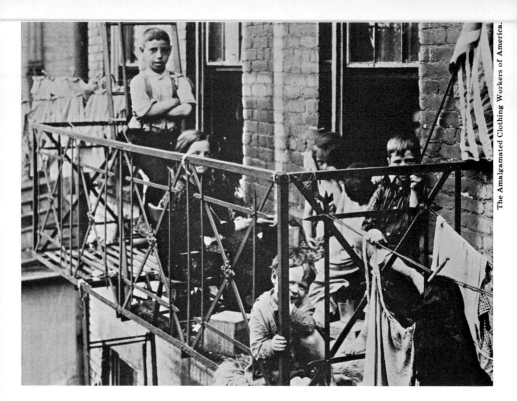

Above
The fire escape had many uses
for tenement dwellers.

Below
A family crowded into
a New York City tenement flat
is seen in this photograph
taken in 1910.

Above
Women garment workers toil
in an East Side workshop, 1905.

Below
Clothing being manufactured
in a Lower East Side sweatshop,
about 1912.

Above
Pushcarts and patrons
on the Lower East Side.

Below
Sweet Potatoes.

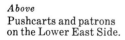

Temporary morgue set up
where relatives could seek to
identify bodies of girls killed
in the Triangle fire.

The fire escapes and
pushcarts of Hester Street,
about 1905.

Above
David Kessler,
star of the Yiddish theater.

Below
Abraham Cahan,
editor of the *Jewish Daily Forward*
and of several novels, including
The Rise of David Levinsky.

Jacob P. Adler,
a giant of the Yiddish theater
and head of the "royal family"
of that theater.
He was the father of
Celia, Stella, Jack, Luther,
and Frances Adler.

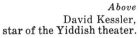

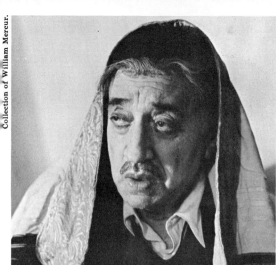

Above
Maurice Schwartz,
founder of the Jewish Art Theater
and a leading star, as he appeared in
I. J. Singer's *The Brothers Ashkenazi.*

Tragedienne Bertha Kalish,
who starred in the Yiddish theater
and went on to Broadway

Below
Playwright Jacob Gordin,
the leading writer of the Yiddish theater
and author of *The Jewish King Lear.*

The Roskolenko
family, 1905.
Edna,
Mother, Esther,
Herschel, Father.

his town. And since all things were normal, including the buying of my first suit, my father soon had a glass of schnapps in his hand and the merchant and he were toasting to some vague past in a variety of toasting languages. It sounded better in Yiddish than it did in Russian. But they toasted me and my first suit, as well. And to make me part of the *landsman* process, I was given a small schnapps—to equal out my sudden relationship to everything that was taking place or about to happen.

The ritual had its own preserves of economics and psychology; for the schnapps, or my thimble of it, would guarantee my silence. What would a boy know about bargaining? I could not intrude when both of them talked about the Ukraine, the *shtetl*, their friends and relatives alive and dead, the union my father belonged to, or the burial society—the *verein*, that would bury him one day in 1937.

I was not quiet. It had to be a blue suit, I said noisily above the ringing sounds the schnapps made in my ears. There was some ambivalent agreement about the color. Not black, not half-blue, not gray—*blue*, I kept saying. My father nodded along with his *landsman* friend of 1895. I nodded to another nod from them. Suits were brought out. A dozen lay on a table. My father, a *mavin*—an expert—on materials, sneered heavily. I sneered lightly, by familial consent. Out came another dozen—to make a tailor's circus of the blue suits piled on two tables. From the mass of suits one finally fitted my blue blueprint—and now the myth and the game began.

"What is the talking price?" my father asked.

Another schnapps passed hands.

"Thirty dollars," said the owner.

My father drank the schnapps, then answered, "Are you mad? For such a small suit and for such a small boy?"

My father had a lovely smile when he was not angry. But he was between anger and a smile. He went on, "I will give you five dollars. And no more schnapps, please."

Another schnapps. More talk about old friends. The suit was completely forgotten. Then, suddenly, it came back . . .

"This is ridiculous!" barked the *landsman*-owner. Then he

95

HARRY ROSKOLENKO

roared, had a quick schnapps himself, offered me another spoon of one—and laughed. "Why, I paid twenty-eight dollars myself, Berel. Twenty-eight dollars, *landsman*."

"For a suit that has been in the store for two years? I know the style, *landsman*. Five dollars, Chaym," insisted my father.

"I must make an honest profit, Berel."

"How honest?" My father rolled two cigarettes. The owner had a hand out.

"How honest? What a question to ask, Berel! How much should I make on a suit for a small boy? You tell me."

"An honest profit will bring my offer up to five dollars and fifty cents, Chaym."

It was prolonged, agitated, and wearisome. We were soon walking out, saying good-bye to the *landsman* who owned all the suits. We were rushed right back when my father, in almost religious tones, said, "Chaym, five dollars and seventy-five cents— and another schnapps, please."

They embraced. I was embraced. I was given, along with my father, a small schnapps. The blue suit was wrapped up, a hanger put into the package—almost one hour after entering the store. We left with the bulking package in my right hand— my first suit.

Outside, ten feet away, I vomited up the schnapps. My emotions, the bargain, all the *landsman* greetings—all went into my first economic reality.

It was that sort of street—a basement on another surface; an enchanted mountain of goods, voices, harangues, anger, stealth, heart, charity, nobility, at its lowest, or highest, for the poor. It was a pious place, too, and efficiently human; a street of many strident banners. It could not have worked in any other way for the people on Orchard Street. The bargains were illusions, at best; or extraordinary, when they were really bargains. The street confused everybody; for it was impossible to know who was the teacher of economics and who was the pupil.

Both had seen the Statue of Liberty one day on their steerage

96

passage to Ellis Island. They had arrived with numbers on their lapels and they spoke every European tongue. They had contrived enough of Orchard Street English to Americanize part of their mind. They had arrived sick, almost dead, to be met by relatives and *landsleit*, and Orchard Street became their natural enough habitat a few weeks later.

Poor, wearing patches like so many Turkish peasants, they soon learned that the country had more than patches—especially on Orchard Street. It had books, clothing, newspapers. Old World things, New World inventions and ways of making money that no one had thought up before—with economic forms that would, despite the street's savagery, add to their citizenship-in-being. It was a new time and another country to all of them; and, like the statue they had seen in the harbor, liberty was all over Orchard Street's garbage and baggage.

But what was this unusual economy based on? It came from massive supplies of shoddy goods—mostly; leftovers from other years and seasons; things that could not be sold uptown, where the better things were; and it was manufactured, after all considerations, for the peddlers and the peasants and the proletarians jamming the sidewalks and gutters. It had been hauled by strong backs, by weak horses, by conceits of value— to the ghetto within the pushcarts. Poor peddlers vied with richer merchants. One yelled higher than another. Prices were cut into all sorts of shapes as all of them argued. Nothing went up but everything went down. Everything had to be sold—and would be, by the wizards with the carts. That was the way it went as thousands of Russians, Hungarians, Polish and Austrian Jews went out with a few dollars to buy up a small segment of Orchard Street's fantasias in goods, food, and frenetics. The transition to richness went from peddling on your bent back with a sack, to a cart, and then, one day, to a store.

Poverty was something all-embracing and too inhuman. But it was so common that we thought nothing of it—except that it was sadder being poor than being rich. The rich were looked up to as noblemen even in the accepted democracy of the streets.

HARRY ROSKOLENKO

Often they came to Orchard Street for some minor slumming, and then, as if they had an advance guard of strong-arm heroes, a passage was created for their coming and going. When they entered a store, ostensibly to look for their own bargains, mobs of poor shoppers would gather outside to speculate on who they were, what they were, whether they were someone's rich relatives doing charity work, or just the rich come to give the poor a little show of contempt for everything that we had or did not have. And since the Orchard Street citizens were not exactly well brought up, a tomato might just as soon be thrown by some small boy who felt aggrieved at the sight. It was a give-and-take affair after the tomato landed where it was supposed to land—on the gentleman's red face.

The women were big-breasted, big-rumped, big everywhere. The black bread or corn bread they habitually ate if they were Jewish created some awesome sexual reveries for us. They would, too, nurse their babies in front of our eyes by merely pulling out the left or the right breast, a nipple to the fore, and into some small mouth it went. If we thought anything, it was very private and most mysterious. Nursing with complete disregard for privacy was done at home as well as in the streets. It was public and normal, though often a more modest woman would put a handkerchief over her huge breast as her child suckled. But the most engaging of the Orchard Street breast-feeders were the Italian women. Darker, larger, eating spaghetti instead of black bread to help enlarge their mammary glands, they gave off more mystery, though hardly as much as the wandering Gypsy women. The Gypsy women were big-skirted, many-skirted, with gold flashing from their teeth to their wrists.

We knew, through all the local folklore, that the Gypsies stole your eyes even as you were looking at them. They threw off a mixture of mayhem and exoticism at the same time—and you were totally enchanted by their balances of magic and thievery. We were warned endlessly never to step into their store-front homes to have our fortunes or misfortunes read. Who had anything worth finding out on Orchard Street? Would it have been

98

the price of old cake, stale for two weeks, that went up for the begging and the bidder? So we looked at the Gypsies, thought all sorts of wayward thoughts, and went on to other economical and social problems—like the price of marinated herring at the store on the corner of Rivington and Orchard.

These conglomerate street bargains had a variety of prices— depending on the age, the smell, the look, and certainly the taste, for you were offered a taste of everything edible and not edible. Milk sold for two cents a quart, with your own pitcher. It was ladled out of 40-quart cans that were not too clean. It was done in a splash by the husband or the wife, depending on who was nearest to the huge milk cans. It was, supposedly, certified and pasteurized—whatever pasteurized meant to me in those days. It must have occurred to me that the cows had been walking about in a pasture—I was that much of a farmer and agriculturist. Butter, smelling a bit rancid, sold for five cents a pound —smell and all. Bread, a cent a pound; but if you wanted a half of a pound it was cut for you from a huge round bread weighing over twenty pounds.

Potatoes, sacked, were bought to make the winter viable. Nobody bothered to buy a pound of potatoes. Potatoes came in sacks weighing fifty pounds—and off we went, father and sons, carrying the sack ten blocks to home. Prunes, plums, tangerines—all of our fruits—came in round crates, and similarly were hauled off home. The difference between prices when buying in bulk and buying in small amounts was something that made bankers of all of us on Orchard Street—the earliest street of bulk and container packaging done in a hurry. As for grapefruits, nobody trusted them yet. They were a bastard fruit, as tomatoes once had been. My mother called tomatoes "love apples"—whatever that must have meant to her. I thought tomatoes were invented to throw at the rich or the street-corner politicans around Election Day.

The herring fleet on Orchard Street was an area devoted to the enormous barrels of brine containing herring from every part of the world. These barrels stood, just below Rivington Street, in the glory of their own odors. There was herring from Holland and Germany. There was pickled fish from Poland, and, of course, from Fulton Street. You came by holding your mother's hand or her big shopping bag made of oilcloth. The bag was cavernous, capable of containing fifty pounds of herring, potatoes, huge amounts of black bread, smoked fish, red cabbage for the borsht—a mammoth collection of the week's food all slopped into one shopping bag. The herrings were wrapped, as a rule, in Yiddish newspapers; much as if the herring business was merely a literary adjunct. For the herring buyers would scan the sheet about to go around the herring. They would make some comment about last week's news, point excitedly to an item that brought them back to Russia or Poland, and soon the wrapped herring was buried in the oilcloth bag and the Yiddish newsprint.

There were the pushcarts and stores of the hats, and hats came in straw, cloth, or various seasonal materials. But it was the caps, with their large visors, that made us, as boys, aware of our infinite ignorance of how to dress. The bigger the visor the tougher you were supposed to be. Nobody went bareheaded in those days; that is, nobody but the intellectuals of East Broadway working on the Yiddish newspapers as reporters, poets, or storytellers. We went hat-headed, nonintellectual, wearing our caps at home as we sat down for our meals; for it was forbidden to be bareheaded while eating . . . and so the trip to the pushcarts of the hats, which we made once a year, was almost a religious visit. We wore the same caps to the synagogue; for few of us had *yarmulkes* as children. Now Christian politicians use *yarmulkes* when campaigning. They are worn by Christians about to incorporate Judaism into their spiritual, if not political, ecumenical circumnavigations. As for the caps, they hung over our heads, eyes and ears, making us resemble so many Jackie Coogans looking for a part in a Chaplin film.

There were the pushcarts of the shoes. Here the shoes were laid out, highly polished, buckled, laced, ready for somebody's dirty

socks. Every cart had a few folding chairs—and you sat on one
of these and went through dozens of attempts to get the right
size, trying them, walking on a carpet for ten feet, coming back
to the chair, sitting down again, your face pinched as much as
your feet. Then another pair was pushed onto your feet. The
shoes we wore then were full shoes, not half. The buttoned ones
had a buttonhook—and it took time to make you an expert but-
tonhooker, especially with the impatient peddler of shoes who
was beyond exasperation after twenty-four attempts to fit you.
Eventually you were shod; but you did not wear your shoes home.
These shoes were for the Jewish holidays. You wore your old
shoes, happily unpinched, except when the Passover came. Then
the new shoes joined the blue suit for a few weeks of high style
on the Holy Days.

There were the carts of the pants sellers, where you could not
try on a pair of knickers, or longies when you were old enough
for the wearing of long pants. At the carts you merely juxta-
posed and aligned your body—for the harried fit. In the stores,
with other kids and their mothers watching, you undressed down
to your underwear to try for more exactness in the fit. When
buying underwear you undressed completely; for in the winter
our parents bought us the heavy winter combinations, John L.
Sullivans, that went from your shoulders to your ankles. A suit
of winter underwear had two logical openings—where they belonged. You wore your winter underwear for two weeks, sleeping in it, stinking a bit at school, and a fortnight later, by economic pateralism, it finally went into a huge laundry bag heading
for the wet wash laundry. You also had but two pairs of long
black stockings for your knickers; and the two pairs made up
your stockings for the year from the Pushcarts of the Stockings.
By the time you were fully adorned from Orchard Street's bargains you were a young animal loosed upon the ghetto's furies
and comedies.

We knew of Little Italy below Greenwich Village and Italian
Harlem, though none of us dared wander to these foreign countries. It was a long walk that ended in a fight when a Jew wan-

101

dered there, and a bloody nose bled better and longer in those days—when pollution did not clog your nostrils. When we did go, it was in gangs; not so much to fight, but to see the strangers up there. Little Italy near the Village was another sort of world to us—darker and just as ugly with tenements. However, it was much more colorful than our world because of the wash hanging on the millions of intersecting clothes lines. Red pants, green skirts, pink shirts—as multicolored as Joseph's coat, which we would not have worn on Cherry Street because we were much more conservative. Our imagination was too orthodox, and it bedeviled me to see the great color arrangements on the clothes lines. I wore only white shirts and blue suits—like a permanent ad for a nonending Bar Mitzvah.

What complex fantasies and distinctive virtues! Economic determinism plus an effective Yiddish, made reality all the more magical—though it always managed to reverse itself. Then fantasy was all you were left with when you had little money for shopping; when my father was out of work, or striking, which was often during the days when the unions, especially the future Cloak Makers Union, and the ILGWU were being organized. Then Orchard Street did not exist. It was ten blocks from home but a no man's land when my father had no pay check to hand over to my mother. Then I stole the little essentials, like candy, from the collection of pushcarts specializing in old candy on the corner of Rivington and Orchard Streets.

In a world of strong smells, odors had many social relationships. Perfume worn by girls and women made them whores. Clean soap made them pure. Hot water did the same. Cold water made you cold, not clean. No water at all made you a dog, not a cat; for cats were always licking themselves. But the strong smells on Orchard Street made every fantasy our instinctive playground; then pushcarts became tag points in all the running games that were inspired by the availability of stolen candies. But to bathe, to swim, to roll in tons of water, there was the swimming pool on Rivington Street—and to get there you had to skirt Orchard Street, steal a little bit, then take a swim for nothing in the public pool. And it was a big holiday if you did not happen to get your nose broken by the street gangs that took over the pool on the day you wanted to go for a swim.

Orchard Street made you a walker and a carrier of many burdens, though candy was not one of them. It also taught you how to run a hundred yards, two hundred yards, then a qaurter of a mile—to escape the wrath of some gang operating on Orchard Street when you had entered, if innocently, their domains of taste—for candy. There was, too, then, the beginnings of juvenile protectionism, usually practiced on some old man who was incapable of enforcing the legalisms of the law around his battered pushcart. Then, either Italians, or Jews, would move in on the poor old man and demand, usually with some minor success, candy—or else. The *or else* meant throwing over his pushcart and running before the cops came to beat the hell out of any of the kids caught operating their junior Mafia on the Elders of Zion's Orchard Street.

Memory is an all-persuasive, primitive magnet. I recall signs, aged when I first saw them, painted thirty years earlier—period-piece signs that hung outside stores on Orchard Street, and not because the owners were trying to charm their customers by aesthetic nuances. They were there because they had been painted, hung, and then forgotten about. One sign at 48 Hester Street read "H. L. Litzky." Were the initials H and L for names like Howard and Lester? It must have been initials for Hyman and Leybel; good enough names for Jews in 1900, though hardly passing in 1971. *Too Jewish*, somebody with 1971 sideburns would say today. The original man with the 1900 vintage sideburns would have thought you insane to have called him any other name than *Hyman*, which in Hebrew is *Chaim*, standing for "life."

The store signs, related as they were to the times, had typical Jewish names, however, for the more Jewish the name the more Jewish the customer. I recall one, Levi Schwartz & Company— whatever *company* meant to me. Begun before the century as a bakery for the local population, it soon had another horde of

103

buyers for its bread, cakes, bagels, bialies—everything in the Jewish baking tradition. It was a company with stores spreading throughout the city; a name . . . and so many companies had begun just like that. There was Breakstone, across from my house at 362 Cherry Street, sellers of dairy products. Breakstone consisted of just one building that smelled of rotting cheese, rancid butter, ancient eggs, milk that had turned sour and was sold— before or after it turned—for a summer delicacy. Breakstone also made *smetana*—which we, as Russian Jews, loved naturally. All the Breakstone products were sold on Orchard Street—after they had aged or smelled their way up there—for a fraction of their original value. It was just another store to us then. In a few years a new millionaire emerged from these dairy products.

The store where my blue suits came from in the pushcart world of woe and bargains was to become famous, later, as the store where the best-dressed men on the Lower East Side, and some actors from Broadway, went to be measured for suits. It acquired a national name that made still another millionaire from Orchard Street's acres of burgeoning merchants. For any voice, literally, was a voice readying the hawker for another haven; another economic empire in the process of jawing up from the badgering streets. Pennies, nickels, dimes, quarters, half dollars—all made an empire, in time. The hoarse voices wheedling the walkers, with lamentable echoes, were to become merchants of glory. They would move away in time from the dirt and garbage, to the greener areas of Long Island and Westchester—wherever the *nouveau riche* Jews went to become Reformed Jews, half Jews, full Jews, half Gentiles, in soul and spirit. But they would have moved also from a street that had a soul that was unique in all its measures, images, sounds, and folk qualities; where a dollar was only half of the image emerging from the shrill compressions of the world's busiest bargains for the poor.

The ghettos of Europe had prepared everybody on Orchard Street to bargain for everything that a house and a home needed. Europe had been the salient school—from a migration, to a sense

104

of not quite belonging anywhere. But the New World, congested, ghettoized by natural design, brought out intimate values that could not have been realized in any other country or any other city. The Lower East Side's many-faceted minds and hearts threw up some social characterizations of the poor. The area contained everybody's universal poverty. Beyond that dismal state of wretchedness, one could only go upward, with wit and humor; and it was Jewish humor, adrift amid the pushcart world that gave off, with princely quavering, the piety of regal Judaism. There was, we knew, a little bit of God with the peddlers and the price of everything on Orchard Street.

Dante's Hell had its sentimental regions of the damned; but Orchard Street had its own variations on the Inferno. It was man-made hell, street-sized, congestion on congestion, hell on hell, the poor on the poor in the great intermingling of accents, faces, bodies, and smells. It was all-American even in the persecutions practiced by the easily corrupted police who harassed the peddlers daily. I do not mean the apple-pickers and their comic byplays, whom we recall from old films, strolling about looking for largess. It was a lot more brutal when a cop took a dollar from a peddler to let him peddle. He took part of a man's life in those days. But it was accepted. It was part of the bargain. It was not Russian barbarism or tsarist persecution. It was Orchard Street's bargains amid the bigger bargains. And many a peddler stayed in business because the man with the blue uniform took his dollar per man and called it American democracy.

You sold, you bought, and you bribed. There was nothing overly sociological or complex about all the modes and arrangements to keep alive. In hell you need cold water, ice, cooling systems, and belief. On Orchard Street you needed to be superhuman as well as mystical, to indulge every type of familial and tribal cunning; to participate in the commercial excitements; to know the heights of envy and the depths of the dollar. It was a unique place for every sort of martyrdom; a nightmare of pushcarts rising up to greet the Lord with thousands upon thousands of people elbowing their way toward Jerusalem, at 50 percent off the retail price. Your pushcart made you an entrepreneur, a handler of commissions, a merchant of no means, a man who knew the secondhand combinations of moral and economic cunning. You lived with a children's bank built into your cartwheels. You had a back that no camel or bull had, for carrying everything on the street. But the margins were there to ready a man for the hinterland beyond Orchard Street—America west of the Hudson River.

There were other streets nearby that had another sort of flair and color, especially Allen Street. It was as exotic as it was erotic with secrecy, darkness, Arabic, Syrian, and Greek music, all of it intermingling with the smell of teas and coffee. The stores sold copper pots, samovars, and candlesticks for the blessing of the Sabbath bread, the fish and the wine, turning Allen Street into a Judaic-Arabic Casbah of the senses. The copperware hung from strings, hangers, windows, in and out of the stores. In the stores, seated, quiet, ancient, were men smoking hookahs, which we, in all of our innocence and Judaism, thought were opium pipes. But many were smoking that too—for it was not exactly illegal then, and nothing much was done about it, we soon learned. We knew of the addicts—and we were satisfied that they were not our own people. They were Chinese, or actors, or whores, or gamblers—and that was enough for our moral references.

But Allen Street was a strange street. It was as much Romanian as it was Greek and Arabic. There were Jewish restaurants for the Hungarian-Romanian Jewish cuisine—heavier, spicier—and you ended up as a fat man. The Greeks and Arabs sold leaner dishes. The Gypsies there sold your future, very thin. There were halvah, sesame seeds, dates, figs, pictures of Muhammad, pictures of Christ, pictures of fat women with their breasts in view—and the entire mixture went along with candies from Egypt, the carpets from Persia—and the whores that walked on Allen Street . . . for everything was tolerated there. Vice was normal on Allen Street. . . .

Over the stores, one flight up, were the coffeehouses of the

106

Greeks, Syrians, and Arabs. They offered up coffee, cognac, and belly dancers—and the bigger the belly the greater the applause. The bigger the bottom the greater the pandemonium. The cafés one flight up were out of bounds for Jews, especially for kids my age, but we managed to rush up, dash in, have a look, see a belly wiggling, huge breasts going in every direction—and out we were thrown. It was all belly and noise, all smoke and choking, all animated—and overly exciting for our young eyes. We heard castanets, drums, singers. A few men were reading newspapers. Some were smoking hookahs. Others were playing checkers. It was a grab-bag of bottoms, games, newspapers—and vibrant melodies . . . for we were away, with cups thrown at us as we tumbled down the stairs.

More than several types of sin were up one flight, we knew . . . and we guessed, Biblical with thoughts, how Sodom and Gomorrah had closed in so close to Orchard Street which was so Yiddish, so pure, so far away from hell and so close to heaven—with bargains in everything physical and spiritual. Nirvana was on Allen Street where the bellies wiggled into the night—but we were part of Orchard Street's many bargains.

Chapter 7
Headlines on East Broadway– the Yiddish Press

In 1971, leaning into the last third of this century's all-engulfing achievements in our varied cultures, there were but three Yiddish daily newspapers left in New York City—yet once, not too long ago, a Jewish immigrant's daily reading could make up eight newspapers, if he sat about a café long enough. For they were on the racks and they came with the tea, coffee, and strudel as vast exercises in dramatic journalism and political acumen. Today, with a crisis every second for everybody, the tea drinker —and he no longer drinks tea in a café, but Scotch at a bar— can read what is left of Yiddish journalism's debacle. *The Forward*, Socialist, with 75,000 readers left, in 1924 had a circulation of 220,000. *The Day-Journal*, liberal, which had, at its height, 105,000 concerned, literary, political, and philosophical readers, today has but 50,000. And the all-engaging document of Stalinism, the *Freiheit*, comes out now but five times a week, with scarcely 7,000 readers, but during the height of Stalin's influence in the thirties its readers numbered many thousands more. But if the debacle in Yiddish journalism does not sound dramatic enough consider that between 1872 and 1917 there were more than 150 periodicals appearing in Yiddish. Most of them are gone along with their readers—workers, scholars, kibitzers, politicians, tea drinkers, businessmen, poker players, union officials, rabbis, students, journalists—and any and every Jew who took pride, once, in his Yiddish mother tongue—his *mama-loshn.*

In 1913, when I was six, I helped my mother sell two of the three papers that now remain—for *The Freiheit* came out later. As a newsboy, who was both stationary and wandering, I knew the mass of Yiddish newspapers and the journals intimately, for they provided various sorts of profit—financial, political, and personal, for my family and me. With my mother, I was able to make about five dollars a day for many hours of slugging around the East Side, getting beaten by the Irish, catching colds, being rained on—when not pissed on by horses. The horses, nonreaders, merely splashed away as I was dodging a truck to get to an old man who looked like an unmovable customer. When I was stationary at the synagogue's newspaper racks and boxes that we had on the corner of Madison and Montgomery Streets, the horses were no longer splashing me in nature. I was just a busy boy calling out headlines, bylines, sponsoring this writer or that writer—anybody who had, that day, written something imposing about us Jews, here and abroad.

Soapboxes, milk boxes, whiskey boxes, made up the ten that paraded along an iron fence to the left of the synagogue's narrow brown doors and the hundreds of papers were piled upon the boxes. Tall racks, with a covering for rain, were laced to the fence for permanence; something my father, in his craftsmanship and zeal, created against the meanderings of thieves and junk merchants.

On these racks were many periodicals—*The Hebrew Standard,* a magazine devoted to contemporary Jewish affairs; *The Maccabean,* Zionist; *The Young Judean,* religious; *The Big Stick,* satirical; *Die Zukunft,* socialist-literary; *Der Freie Arbeiter Stimme,* anarchist; and dozens of others. Then came the big daily papers hurriedly piled on the boxes according to their headlines and disposability: *The Day, The Jewish Daily News, The*

110

Morning Journal, The Forward—which had the largest box—
and the *Warheit,* which had the smallest one. And to make five
dollars a day from penny papers and five-cent magazines made
us mathematical magicians as we counted, over and over, hundreds of pennies, during one of the piquant interludes that occurred between those rushing us to get into the synagogue and
those rushing us to get to the trolleys and to their jobs.

Everybody we knew was in the same condition—poor; but the
newer immigrants envied the older ones, though both had come
from the same abysmal villages, towns, and cities, with little to
envy: kitchens without running water; toilets in the fields or
the back yards; a primitive world where the word *zhid* or *yid*
ran along with every other curse as a normal greeting. But in
front of the synagogue, on the Lower East Side, things were more
humanly viable. It was another country and another time—for
Jews . . . and the newspapers were telling them, in Yiddish
journalism, about the better times they were in and what would,
with some certainty, happen the day after the day after. For as
the People of the Book, they were, by their self-assertive inheritance, now the people of the Yiddish newspapers. They mingled
in shops, streets, and societies, arguing their way through their
favored writers and their cartoonists. Bosses, politicians, and the
tsar were always cartooned. There were lyrical poems—about
the skies and the sweatshops; stark, brooding, addressed to the
man going into the synagogue—to pray in a hurry. When he
left, with a newspaper, he was a socialist on his way to his job,
where the essence of poetry ran out of him for twelve hours a
day—as sweat.

A man either had God or socialism or he was in business; but
then, with some intellectual and psychological variants, he could
be involved in all three and not feel contradictory. It was the
nature of the Yiddish press, hardly beholden to heroic images,
to have no servitors. For consistency, there was a Yiddish question mark. One day a writer, much read and respected, would
come out for Populism, favoring Theodore Roosevelt and his
Bull Moose Party; the next, he would be opposed, favoring pure
socialism without any eccentric sociopolitical alterations. An-

other writer, equally gifted for his honor and virtue, would come out favoring dogs—then doing excellently, along with the horses, in the streets. Three days later the same journalist, fed up with the slow trolleys, would debate a journalist of another paper about the virtues of buses, run by engines, not by horses, to get a worker to where he wanted to go—and not take all morning. And workers wanted to go many places: to work, to the cafés, to meetings, to Second Avenue, to Goldberg's Farm in Brooklyn— by subway; to Queens, to the cemeteries, by trolley or subway to cry a little over a grave; or to the ocean and to the rolling air —away from the toxic gutters of his ghetto.

The Yiddish press was the immigrant's moral arbiter. It was public as well as private with its news and tales. It was each reader's own paper, addressed to him alone—the man who happened to spend one penny—much as if it had been written entirely for him and was sponsoring all of his immediate *tsuris* as an East European lost on East Broadway's wide circus of the heart.

The Jewish press began in New York in 1832, when a periodical called *The Jew*, printed in English, proselytized against Christian missionaries trying to turn Jews into Christians— both failing, soon enough, by common default—and its few Jewish readers continued to remain Jews. In 1849, another weekly, *The Asmonean*, took up the cultural and religious problems arising among the earlier English-reading Jews, and for ten years literary essays by the editor, Robert Lyon, dealt with the soul and the spirit of the Jews in New York City's burgeoning cultures awaiting moral identification. After that, in 1857, came *The Jewish Messenger*, which had a basic Orthodox message and lasted until 1903, when orthodoxy was being challenged by German-created Reform Judaism . . . and since orthodoxy had a longer journalistic imprint, starting during the Civil War, when Jonas Bondy edited *The Jewish Record*, the competitive reformers as against the ritualistic affirmers locked horns, in and out of the synagogues.

There were, later, *The American Hebrew* and *The Hebrew Standard*, both orthodox weeklies; *The American Jewess*, cultural, begun in 1895, as a quarterly; *Helpful Thoughts*, for housewives who wanted advice on more than cooking *kreplakh* and making *tsimes*. But soon more solid journals appeared. *The Maccabean*, Zionist and timely, was concerned with another land, much more ancient than Manhattan Island. It wrote about the immigrant Jews turning to another sort of nationalism—to Palestine, to their Biblical heritage, to plan their lives with their own people, in the land of Israel. After that came the first national Jewish magazine, *The American Jewish Chronicle* . . . and on and on, turning past the new century, vying with each other in scholarship and influence, taking up the Jewish affairs of the entire nation rather than the ghettos of New York's many dilemmas.

The past and the present were commingling now. In New York, coming into another age, with another language working out our needs, Jews were confronted by more than synagogue values. Many held on to their past and others went into new trades, into commerce, into the professions.

For many thousands of Jewish immigrants, the pressing iron and the sewing machine were developing a new industry—the clothing industry in big lofts and small lofts, with cockroaches and lions all selling their labor skills and their merchandising techniques. The things of flotsam and the gestures of money mangled the emerging man, the owners; or their workers, in their unions. The questing masses and the bosses both had their Yiddish newspapers to tell them what they were doing, industrially and spiritually—and where it would lead to, in the end.

It was the Jewish press that welcomed the Jewish migrating masses. Yiddish was a language of journalism that was indeed new to new America, but old, for those who could read, in Eastern Europe. There it had come into its own as a wanderer's speech, picking up, after its basic German, words in Russian, Polish, Romanian, Hungarian—and the related words and sounds that came with the borrowings of many tongues. Each country had added special words or words had been altered by accents, to merge with the Yiddish created during the Middle Ages—and to add confusion as well as cohesion to East Broadway's variegated readers of Yiddish. On the wide streets were editors, satirists, playwrights, novelists—and working journalists, often the same people.

A poet, too, was always a journalist—in order to make some sort of living, when he was not, too often, working in a factory. He had come with a *shtreimel* and a *peltz*, but he gave up the religious hat and fur coat of the older ghetto and was wearing what was being made in America, on the industrial frontiers of Manhattan, in the lofts and shops.

No matter what a man did, it was done with accents, flavors, and gusto in his speech. It was a Yiddish of many variations and humor that one Jew spoke to another, and what they said dealt with what they did. For belief came in two ways—via religion and politics.

The first adventure in Yiddish journalism started in 1872 with *Die Jüdische Post*, edited and set by hand by Henry Gershuni— a latter-day Ben Franklin—but hardly reaching the standards or longevity of the *Saturday Evening Post*. Other weeklies, other failures, other conceits—and then in 1874 came the weekly *Jüdische Gazetten*, which ran for half a century and was published by one of the most enterprising editors of that period, Zwi Sarasohn, who had tried, earlier, with German and Hebrew periodicals, equally orthodox. Sarasohn was, in 1885, to create the first Yiddish daily, the *Tageblatt*—Conservative, Orthodox, concerned with immigrant affairs—and it was to become the model for all the newspapers that followed. At last a Yiddish daily had found a permanent audience.

But the real level of social and political thinking began with *Das Abendblatt*, the Socialist Labor Party's official Yiddish paper, and authoritarian Daniel De Leon's organ for revolutionizing the new proletariat arriving via steerage daily in 1894. But the paper ceased in 1902 as the result of a political death inspired by the split-away Socialist Party, which emerged from the more radical Socialist Labor Party in 1897. *The Forward*, founded in 1897, with Abraham Cahan editing what was to become the most famous Yiddish paper in the world, would herald the new party, the new green cousins in their alleys and tenements, in a Yiddish they could understand, with popular features like *"Bintel Brief"*—published letters on all sorts of personal subjects—which inspired some readers to write even more subjective letters. This feature was totally original, tear-jerking, sentimental, comical, making you cry and laugh at love affairs, divorces, abandoned mothers, business failures, religious differences, and poverty. Every letter, no matter how illegibly scrawled, that was put into an envelope and addressed to *The Forward*, 175 East Broadway, was read by Abraham Cahan. The paper went all over the States as well as to Canada, South America—and to Eastern Europe—to the countries many of the letter writers had abandoned, bringing unique messages from the New World to the Old. There were answers, too, from European relatives, shocked at the morals of their relatives on the Lower East Side.

New papers were born, and as the Jews of New York reached political and social sophistication, they took their stand on many issues of the day. *The Jewish Morning Journal*, the first Yiddish morning paper, in 1902 reached a circulation of 108,502 religious Jews, businessmen, sensation-mongers, and ordinary gossipers. Three years later, in 1905, Yiddish journalism was to get its first unusual journal—a personal paper, *The Jewish Daily Warheit*, published by Judge Aaron J. Levy. The *Warheit* was radically democratic, national in scope, politically competitive, right behind *The Forward* in circulation, and challenging it for labor adherents, with the judge's legal and bombastic opinions extremely obvious in the reportage and editorials.

Papers began and suspended, with fickle readers going on to other new papers. There was the German-Jewish *Yiddische Welt* —out to make Americans in a hurry, which lasted from 1902 to 1904. Its editor, Lewis E. Miller, had a long history as a newspaper-starter and burier. He was to start the *Abend Zeitung* in 1906 and kill it in ninety days . . . and just as World War One

115

broke out Mr. Miller would try again, this time with a Yiddish paper called *Der Führer*. This lasted eighty-nine days despite its pro-Russian sympathies, as, for example, attacking the Kaiser, which was hardly popular in 1914 among the Jewish proletarians, who were for attacking the Tsar.

Finally, *The Day* came in 1914, and it is still here as *The Day-Journal*. By 1917, having changed the soul of its first editorials, which were pro-Germany, the paper was thoroughly for the Western Powers and had a circulation of 85,000 objective, most literary, most scholarly readers. Considered a writer's paper, like the earlier *Jewish Daily News*, it was to introduce an English section, hoping to hold its readers, to teach them English—and, eventually, to lose its readers to *The Herald, The World, The New York Times, The Call, The Mail*—when they had learned enough of the language to integrate their citizenship.

The English section of *The Day*, however, made them half as native as the cop and the street cleaner; for with sufficient English a Jew could race into politics with his adopted tongue and become, like the new Poles, Germans, Italians, Slavs—and Jews —half of a talker as well as a reader. He could hold up *The Mail* in the subway and read it to himself. Then, for himself, getting louder, he was pronouncing words he really understood as he acknowledged *The Day's* quaint intellectual services.

But all of those papers were getting heavier for my mother and me. I lifted them, packed them, sold them, hustling about, making my husky shoulders huskier . . . and I began to look like a kid gymnast and wrestler by the time I was eight years old. Then I was no longer attacked by the Irish in my rounds of cafés and coffeehouses as I sold Yiddish-English, or *Yinglish*, as a friend of mine called *The Day's* English reportage.

The ten boxes at our stand soon were not enough and I found another whiskey box for *The Day*. Within a week, since we were now crowding the entrance to the synagogue, the *shammes*—the caretaker—was objecting, not so much to our obstruction but to the new *whiskey* box advertising Scotch.

116

Said the *shammes* to my mother: "It does not look good, that box. . . ."

"How should it look?"

"Not like whiskey. After all, think of the *shul*."

"What has the whiskey box to do with the *shul*? Don't you have a schnapps?"

"One a day, after the evening's *mairev*. But the morning, *g'otenu*!"

"Would an egg box be better?" asked my mother.

"Eggs, milk, anything *milchedig*—but not a schnapps box!"

Of the Yiddish weeklies I sold when I was a boy, the most exciting ones were the freewheeling *Big Stick*, begun in 1909, and *Der Freie Arbeiter Stimme*, which was anarchist from front to back, to center, totally sold on Bakunin, rallying to every cause, free with its huge opinions and small type, high-thinking, but reaching only 12,000 anarchists by 1917 after twenty-seven years of a dolorous, romantic, bohemian life. Last year it celebrated its 80th—as the oldest weekly in the world. And with the forty-four Yiddish periodicals then being published in the United States, eight of them dailies, newspaper selling was as competitive as the cloak industry. For me, however, with competition on every other block and in front of every other synagogue, *The Big Stick*, cosmopolitan in its wit and irony, needled us with cartoons and comic strips, attacking puritans and populists alike, virgins and whores—in politics, linking Samuel Gompers to John D. Rockefeller, who was just as dime-thin then, and had already begun to give out that gentle coin to needy children. *The Big Stick* did not spare anybody, especially sacred socialist calves, cows, and donkeys; nor Theodore Roosevelt, whom it allegedly interviewed regarding the state of the national zoo, Bull Moose in style, in 1909. Tabloid in size, *The Big Stick* hit away at friends much as if they were bitter enemies, establishing some equal disdain for their differences. If the paper liked anybody or anything, it was an unqualified mystery to me . . . but I knew what it did not like, weekly, with its savage kibitzing of

117

the poverty around us. It went after the earlier breed of social workers and sociologists then starting up the newest profession. It was *The Big Stick* way up the human zoo's arse . . . and the city's.

Where are the papers now and the magazines that I sold? In the morgues of Jewish libraries and in the main public library's Jewish branch. Their brittle pages are boxed or tied with string. Fragments fall into the reader's lap. The histories and all the nuances of the immigrant nation's ways are wrapped in large brown envelopes to keep the crumbling pages briefly intact so that one can read, before all of it is microfilmed, what went on sixty and seventy years ago during my father's immigrant days. In the library, men over their beards, falling asleep, waking up, read what they still know or what they forgot from the many Jewish publications that began in 1832, in German, Hebrew, English—and that ended in the language they knew best—Yiddish, as they wipe their glasses and wonder where the entire immigrant culture went.

Yiddish, in Manhattan, is a history within a history. In 1917, just before the Russian Revolution sent more semisettled wanderers wandering again, the Yiddish press had the following circulation:

The Day	65,369
The Forward	148,560
The Jewish Daily News	55,000
The Morning Journal	87,322
The Warheit	50,241

A Jewish statistician adding up the daily runs and the many hands and readers through which each paper passed might, on his way to the synagogue, conclude that there were, yearly, 111,-000,000 readers of these dailies. And if his mind wandered from his prayers and he thought earnestly about the denouement of Yiddish journalism, he would come up with the following table, ending in 1917, for the entire Jewish press:

118

TYPE OF PUBLICATION	LANGUAGE					General Tendency					Jewish Tendency					
	Number Published in English	Number Published in Hebrew	Number Published in Judeo-Spanish	Number Published in Yiddish	Number Published in all Languages	Republican	Democratic	Socialist	Anarchist	Nonpartisan	Orthodox	Conservative	Reform	Zionist	National Radical	Cultural
Dailies	3			5	8	2	1	1		1	2			1	2	
Family Journals			1	3	4						3	1		1	1	
Weekly Party Organs		2		4	6			2	1		1			3	1	
Monthly Party Organs	2			1	3			1						1		1
Professional and Trade Journals	2			3	5											
Trade Union Papers	1			6	7											
General Bus. Papers				1	1											
Organizat'n Bulletins	1			2	3											
Neighborhood Journ's				2	2											
Juvenile Periodicals	2	1		1	4											
Humorous Papers			1	1	2											
Annuals	1				1											
TOTAL	12	3	2	29	46	2	1	4	1	1	6	1		6	4	1

119

HARRY ROSKOLENKO

I was the seller of papers and the reader was in a hurry; I was thus the arbiter of occasional tastes whenever my older, religious brethren were in a hurry. They snatched at anything that I gave them as they rushed into the synagogue, then dashed, ten prayerful minutes later, out to the horsecars to read, enroute to work and at lunch, what the inspired controversial press had to say that day. Often they would argue with my mother, much as if she had written the headlines. They would throw Russian, Polish, German, and Yiddish at her in one blurp of a sentence. They stuck pennies into her good left hand or into mine. All of it made up the five dollars in pennies, nickels, dimes, quarters, half dollars—and an occasional dollar, which we studied for its greener reality.

East Broadway was Yiddish Alley. It was longer than Fleet Street and as square as Park Row, where most of New York's papers were then published. But East Broadway was not merely involved in Yiddish journalism; it was the intellectuals' street, running for so many blocks west, where it became Chatham Square, then east, where it ended suddenly; though a hurried walker, blindfolded, could fall into the East River off Corlears Hook Park. Coffeehouses, private clubs, *vereins*, collection societies for Palestine, rabbinical schools—East Broadway was the sentimental heart and the battling mind of our ghetto. There chiding journalists took each other on over a lunch of herring, black bread, a glass of tea—to insult each other's newspapers, words, ideas, politics, in and out of print. Often they came out of the same building; for many a magazine and newspaper shared the same presses in the cellars. They also shared more than the mechanical equipment—their flats, apartments, summer homes, women, politics, and clothes. For the pay, then, kept a writer as poor as a worker.

Yiddish journalism, at its worst, was a horrendous opera. It had but one purpose—a large quantity of tears. If it had a second, it was more tears. *Di trern* cascaded. But Yiddish, when it was not crying, was on a level of world prose—stemming from the Russian and German classics with storytelling inventiveness.

120

It had a tremendous folklore to borrow from, *fun di velt*—from the world. It was written with wit, sensitive to every edge of word and thought nuances, a Don Quixote-ish language that made guilt, identification, moral myths, exaggeration, and factual history the archer's center—when the arrow reached the heart . . . and the stories and the reportage by Leon Kobrin, Sholem Asch, Abraham Raisin, Sheen Daixel, Jacob Gordin, Peretz Hirschbein, Zalmon Libin, Moishe Nadir, Joseph Opatoshu, Sholem Aleichem, Lamed Shapiro—and so many others, created the journalism, the art, and the extraordinary virtues of a language in being and act.

The growth of New York's Yiddish newspapers, oddly, was the result of the tsar's anti-Semitic policies, the cossacks' whips, the pogroms. Spreading throughout Eastern Europe, anti-Semitism created forced immigration. For without that, how many Jews would have uprooted their old world? Between 1880 and 1914, 2,500,000 Jews came from Europe to the United States—and most read some Yiddish as their mother tongue. From Russia alone a half million Jews left between 1903 and 1908, with 90 percent coming to the United States. Another set of figures, taking in the years between 1900 and 1910, has 1,000,000 immigrants coming to the United States from Russia, with 64 percent remaining in New York. They came and they worshipped—for by 1921 there were 843 synagogues in the city, and many resembled the cellar-store Puerto Rican churches of today in the swamped ghettos where a greenhorn met a *chaver* and life with a friend began again.

My father, a good reader who sat reading for hours after work, the glasses over his forehead, then over his eyes, peering at papers and books, the light from the chandeliered mantles fading, rising, making him look up, would point to *The Morning Journal*, Republican, Orthodox, the server of the community, or so said the paper somewhere between its masthead and its editorials. . . . And my father would remark, "This is a newspaper? This is God's language? This is objectivity?" and he read out to us the

121

account of the assassination of Crown Prince Ferdinand: " 'The Crown Prince was a man with humane feelings . . . who belonged to a dynasty with which we have always had certain sympathies. . . .' "

Uncle Solomon went my father one better and read an editorial from the anarchist weekly, the *Freie Arbeiter Stimme*: " '. . . if the Archduke had not been killed and had become the emperor, there would have begun a period of the worst reaction for Austria which perhaps would have ended only with a people's war.' "

My sister Edna read from the *Tageblatt*: " 'Pan-Slavism is one of the greatest barriers to progress and humanity and a stone in the path of civilization. . . .' "

I asked, "Why a stone? Why not a pebble or a mountain? What kind of a stone—like the Pilgrims' Rock?"

I got several unkind *shhhes* from all. I was intruding again. "What is Pan-Slavism?" I asked my sister.

"Those who favor the Pans—I mean the Slavs," she said, scholarly.

"Who are the Pans—Huns?"

I was told to leave the room. I went to the toilet in the hall and arbitrated with nature. The *shhhes* had made me angry. I was old enough to ask what certain words meant, certainly something as strange as "Pan-Slavism"—which I never favored, after that discussion. I buttoned my fly. I returned. I washed my hands. I sat down with the elders, and took a schnapps—to get my face slapped, but by my sister . . .

"At your age, you drink?"

"Let him have it," said my father. "He'll sleep better, with or without Pan-Slavism."

The war—with the schnapps—had obviously emboldened me. At seven, what would a boy know about wars? I had never seen one, merely read about many romantic wars. Death had something to do with not opening your eyes anymore. I went to sleep. I opened them. I closed them, listening to the talkers, to my sister being the young librarian, reading from her clippings, filing

122

them back, arguing with Uncle Solomon. . . . And I, at school, argued the same. I used their words, remembering their quotations, mangling them here and there, making the excitements of the new war in Europe come into the classrooms. After school, I paraded with my newspapers all the calamities abroad.

The arguments for the war and against it divided Jew from Jew, in painful ways. The newspapers hardly helped to get a cohesive view. Many Jews, though of Russian origin, were against their country of birth. They favored the editorials of *The Morning Journal* and other Yiddish newspapers. They favored Emperor Franz Joseph of the Hapsburg Empire and the Kaiser of Germany, for Franz Joseph, my mother said, "Is a kind man who never troubled the Jews of Austria and Hungary. . . ."

The Kaiser came in for some kind words, too. Germany had a political system that allowed for popular elections—not possible in tsarist Russia. Russia had pogroms, Germany and Austria— never! Germany had great Jewish intellectuals, doctors, scientists, writers—and men in public life. The arguments favoring the Central Powers, then, at my father's living room, were too many—and they were absorbed by me. I got many a juvenile lecture about the soul of man, Jewish, and the nature of war, Christian. Jews never started wars because they did not have a country to make war for . . . and the mysteries of Zionism multiplied. What makes a war? Who makes a war? Was war always for justice? Was it not because of trade, nationalism, colonialism, money, wealth—the world?

The war took over the heart of the Yiddish press daily. It meant death to relatives, friends, close kin. I read about the war early in the morning as my mother and I collected four of the five Yiddish dailies on East Broadway, then went on to 79 Bowery, for *The Morning Journal*. Whatever I read, then, was absorbed in my memory and recalled with the help of my sister's filing furies . . . and I quote from the periodical *The Ladies Garment Worker*, for November 1914: "There are few of us who have not some relative in the affected countries. It is therefore

123

natural that our commiseration for them should be more intense than of people who are not familiar with the sights and scenes of the devastated regions and cannot picture the heartbreaking agony of millions of suffering people.''

I read on, then, from other periodicals. A reporter from the *Warheit*, walking about the ghettos of New York City on July 24, 1914, came across fellow Jews cursing the Tsar and praising Franz Joseph . . . and I read again, a week later, that on Saturday, August 1, 1914, in various synagogues Galician Jews offered up prayers for the Austrian emperor, Franz Joseph; that in the ghettos Jews offered to join the German Army and went to the German Consulate to enlist. The German Consul in New York asked the Hebrew Immigrant Aid Society to shelter the Jewish volunteers until they were ready to embark for Germany . . . and all of this was printed, then, in the *Tageblatt*, once considered objective, politically astute, literary, all-knowing, with the purest conscience of journalism . . . and one day, in 1928, the *Tageblatt* was to disappear.

Neither Uncle Solomon nor my father had any use for the Tsar—for they had both served in his armies. My father carried with him forever the scars and lashes from the *nagaika* across his back. Uncle Solomon had a bad left eye, from a blow . . . and I was getting details, with their memories on memories. Blows! Lashes! Blood on blood!

The *tshanik* was boiling water for tea. My sister was quoting from *The Forward* regarding the war's issues and Jews taking sides. . . . ''Let them thank God they are in America without having to be forced to kill people and die needlessly themselves. . . . It is true that we wish the Russian Czar black defeat in this war. But this is also the wish of his own soldiers. . . . Why should we shoot them?''

It was quotation after quotation. Again from the *Tageblatt*, August 12, 1914: ''The Jews support Germany because Russia bathes in Jewish blood . . . who will dare say that it is a crime for Jews to hate their torturers, their oppressors, their murderers? . . . It is natural that Jewish sympathies should be on the side of learning and not on the side of ignorance.''

124

THE TIME THAT WAS THEN

Natural allies? Natural enemies? From *The Morning Journal*
on September 9, just before I turned seven, I was to read: "We
were persecuted in Russia, forced to leave the land of our birth,
and we have a full moral right to hate our oppressors and to desire
their defeat. It is regrettable that England has placed herself on
Russia's side, and we believe that this was unnecessary. We
would not want to see England go down, and we are certain
that she shall not go down. But she has no business allying herself
with an Asiatic barbarian, and if she shall pay dearly for this,
it will only be a sign that there exists an historical justice. But
we hope that she shall in time wriggle out of her criminal error
and that it shall not cost her dearly. . . . We do not step over
any bounds of neutrality or morality by expressing this wish."

This view was not one-sided—to save England's soul alone.
The French had got it as well from the same paper. On August
3, 1914, an editorial stated:

"The French Republic deserves to be punished for her un-
clean love for Russia, and if she takes her attachment so seriously
as to go to war for her barbaric lover, she shall at the end get
what she deserves."

This was Yiddish journalism as a war broke out. It was within
the battles. It fought for spiritual areas of the past; part pride,
part vengeance, and for the conscience of workingmen who were
Jews. In the *Freie Arbeiter Stimme*, the autocrat of anarchism,
I read on September 24, 1914—after the German invasion of
Belgium: "Why has France forgotten about the Paris Commune
of 1871 and remembered only Alsace-Lorraine?"

The war was to change daily, monthly, yearly—after the emotions awakened by tsarism had run out; when the killing reached
millions on both sides; when socialist theories said that it was a
capitalist war, at best; at worst, the working class, in the
democracies, might come out just as democratic as they went
in. But, nevertheless, why kill for an English king, a Russian
tsar, an Austrian emperor, a German kaiser, or for the democracies that were equally the servitors of capitalism? But the socialist movements had split all around the world, and that included
the Lower East Side. In 1916, Allan L. Benson, the Socialist

125

Party's candidate for President, received 585,113 votes campaigning against militarism and war.

The Forward echoed and reechoed all the political changes on the East Side. When Morris Hillquit ran for mayor in 1917, he received, as he campaigned for a quick peace, 146,000 votes. Seven socialists were elected aldermen and ten assemblymen. But the Socialist Party split the following year, when President Wilson announced his Fourteen Points—to preempt much of *The Forward's* acceptable solutions to end the war.

These were some of the Yiddish papers, New York written, worldwide read, created on East Broadway, sold by my mother and myself when the war broke out. We had relatives in Europe and their letters told us intimately about the death of cousins in the tsarist armies. But this was America and our future was in the streets, shops, offices—and in the synagogue. Our past was in another country, and we would, one day, become equal Americans, giving up Yiddish for the cultures and subcultures of New York's ghettos and nonghettos. Another sound, called Progress, would drum on our ears. Progress meant using English totally and thinking as an American. It meant losing one sort of intimacy and taking up the echoes of another language. Another energy would embrace us, as growing Americans, and Yiddish, so universal as a literature, would fail us. The magazines and newspapers that many hundreds of thousands had read, as immigrants and citizens, would come to the end of their time as vehicles of a pulsating speech. Some facts, some statistics, one day, told us everything. But there would, for sentimental reasons, be a temporary resurgence about Yiddish as a language of joy—without readers, written in English. The old men who had kept some of the press going were gone. In another thirty years, Yiddish would be a language to be studied by scholars—just as the year 2000 began.

Long ago, S. Margoshes, a Yiddish journalist, wrote: "Looking back on the history of the Yiddish . . . press in New York City, one cannot help being struck by the closeness with which it runs parallel to the entire course of Jewish development in New York City. It would seem as if every change in the complexion of New York Jewry would register itself in the Jewish press almost automatically.''

It did, in *The Forward*, and I quote one of its 1916 war statements: ''We have to be Americans. We shall be. We shall learn English. We shall accommodate ourselves to the laws and organization of the country. We shall interest ourselves in her politics. . . . We shall love America and help to build America. We shall accomplish in the New World a hundred times more than we could in the Old.

''But you shall not be able to erase the old home from your heart. The heart shall be drawn elsewhere. And in our solitude, images shall rise up and stare in our faces with eternal sorrow. . . .

''It is difficult to be a Jew in the world. It is much more difficult to be a Jewish immigrant.''

127

Chapter 8
Peddlers and Poets

The first Jew to arrive in New York, then called New Amsterdam, was an Ashkenazi Jew named Jacob Barsimon—a refugee from anti-Semitic Brazil—in 1654. He was not a peddler nor was he a poet. But as a Jew, fleeing from the same sort of thing that had made his forebears flee earlier, he had the poetry of Judaism in him. The peddling was man-made. Social conditions, a strong back or a weak horse, it made no difference—and a man was off with pots and pans, whatever was needed or not needed in the earlier wilderness of the United States. The wilderness, then, began on a track outside the simple cities, flooding into the mud and snow of the then-frontiers of our country.

On the East Side, in my time, the peddlers were universal people. Every beggar, too, was a part-time peddler selling odd lots of garbage. His goods came out of burlap bags, out of pockets—wherever anything could be stuffed. He was a man who had seen the sweatshops and thought they were for someone else. He would peddle, talk, make up stories, enhance his bargains, be the poet of a language that had an inner poetry created into its harshness. All he needed was some magical sounds, shoddy goods, eager eyes, the middle of the gutter, a street corner—and he was speaking his own commentaries, another prophet among other prophets. His real poetry, however, he got in the synagogue. There he listened while the *rov* —the rabbi—or the *chazzen*—the cantor—intoned, sang, and declaimed. It might have been anything from the Song of Songs to a passage from the five books of the Pentateuch—Genesis, Exodus, Leviticus, Numbers, and Deuteronomy; ancient history, laws, admonitions, the songs of Moses—enough to fill your heart and head with spiritual light. But the pushcart poetry was peddled like so many magical words around the ghetto; songs for nothing at all about everything that made up the comedy of a race when it was not too tragic. Both tragedy and comedy were constant, we said, as the People of the Book.

The Yiddish press, which was to publish the future literature, began in 1870. By some bizarre twist, the first Yiddish poet, Meir Rabinovitch, was a ritual slaughterer—a *shochet*—as well as a scribe. He was also a thunderer for God, a *chazzen* who sang in the synagogue. Rabinovitch, just as quaintly, did not use Yiddish themes or Old World sentiments. He wrote about national social problems, including the elections of 1872—which made him the first Yiddish poet laureate, by default.

Meir Rabinovitch was followed by a former rabbi, Yankev Zevi Sobel, from Odessa. Sobel, however, was an involved man. His world was totally Judaic, for he was concerned with the future of an old land called Israel. His first book showed his dedication; for the first poem in it was *The Golden Song of Old Israel*. Another poem, somewhat removed, was *The Polish Scholar in America*. Here the scholar is the peddler out to make enough money to continue his scholarship—and thus the little myth of the poet and the peddler, or the poet and the American peasant, began with Sobel's poem written in 1876.

Behind every broken-down pushcart on Orchard Street, Hester, or Rutgers was a peddler who was a poet first and a peddler when he needed a customer. He wrapped herring—and his comment was saltier than the herring inside the old Yiddish newspaper. The pages were separated, stacked, news of other worlds—not of Orchard Street's wrapped-up bargains and agonies. When the peddler did not specialize in herrings, he sold vegetables—and he was less salty in his comments about his neighbors, his fellow rhetoricians on his left selling beets, worn potatoes, prunes and carrots for *tsimmes,* or half-smashed tomatoes. Everything was second-third-hand, ready for the dogs; nevertheless, human beings were buying it in various tongues—Yiddish from Hungary, Romania, Latvia, Poland, Russia; and the poet-peddler's speech was an amalgam of many biting accents. But no matter how bitter it was you laughed sadly as a poor old woman, somewhat confused, went off with her bedraggled herrings and vegetables.

Paper bags were unknown then. All the brutal bargains went with a single sheet from one of the many Yiddish newspapers, wrapped hurriedly, in an economy where everyone was equal even down to the leaking packages whose wake followed the woman's slow progress. Bargains blended with peddling and poetry on the gallop, in the bedlam, mud, and snow.

Pogroms increased the immigration from Russia in 1881, when the vast tides came into New York's earliest tenements. Along with their few possessions—books, little money, religious objects, bundles of pillows, quilts, and bedding; samovars, old fears in a new world, old world tokens—the Jewish immigrants brought with them the need for an immediate language—English. But the language actually used was Yiddish, instead, or Polish and Russian, for to study English then was difficult for people too old to learn another language. My mother, who arrived in 1895 speaking Russian, Polish, Yiddish, and Hebrew, never learned to speak English. She picked up some simple phrases, all mispronounced with ease, but she continued to speak all the tongues of her childhood, and English to her, forever, was a baffling Anglo-Saxon bewilderment.

But of all the tongues of the Jewish immigrants from Eastern Europe, Yiddish, in every shade and nuance, gave them back the interior poetry they wanted. It spelled itself the way it wanted to—on the basis of your own sounds. If it had a grammar in my

131

youth, I was never to learn it. Such formality was not essential
to its enormous wit and byplays, which made it a sort of earlier
Joycean tongue-of-many-tongues and most natural for poetry,
or peddling to the poor and the rich. It was a folk speech, though
earlier it had been scorned by the elite, but when Moses Mendels-
sohn, the German-Jewish philosopher of the Age of Enlightenment, translated the Old Testament into Yiddish, it became, late
in the eighteenth century, a language of prophecy and poetry.

What my neighbors spoke, what the peddlers harangued with,
what the poets wrote, was Yiddish with a *tam*—a taste. It took
on gestures as they bargained with the bargainers; phrases that
are beyond adequate translation; a language of a ghetto and a
culture that was beyond the pushcart and went into the realms of
metaphysics and mysticism. Some of the plays written in Yiddish, especially *The Golem*, adapted by Leivick, and *The Dybbuk*,
by Ansky, raised the language to astonishing literary and psychological values. This was the language that I heard—witty, all
humor, savage, yet with few real cursing words. It was a language that made you cry, and it always made you laugh—or
both. It was a language of extremes, a poet's language given away
for nothing at the pushcarts.

The Jewish labor movement helped to develop the poets, if not
the peddlers. The first Yiddish literary critic was David Edelstadt, who wrote for the *Freie Arbeiter Stimme*, but though
Edelstadt was arguing textual matters, at the pushcarts they
had every school of criticism; realism, ontological, social symbol-
ism, religious—and with it went herring, potatoes, prophecy—
all wrapped in those single sheets of Yiddish newspapers, circa
1913.

When I was eight, my mother—too busy, one-armed, trying to
run a railroad flat on a timetable with six children in her ears—
would send me off to Hester Street or Orchard Street, wherever
she had heard, that morning, that the bargains were a cent better
on five pounds of potatoes.

On Hester Street there was a tall, Biblical figure; old, gentle
in a sarcastic Yiddish way, literary; a quoter of poetry—and

132

the poetry went with the vegetables. For a dime you came away with poems by Edgar Allan Poe; for a quarter, Shakespeare. I never spent more than a dime—and the old man, on hearing me show off a newly remembered poem by Poe, would immediately translate it back into Yiddish. My memory has erased much of the *tam*; but his face glowed much as if he were Poe about to write "The Valley of Unrest"—with a bottle of rum in one hand and a quill in the other. When the time came to wrap up my potatoes, he would say, "Keep reciting, little boy. I will show you what a literary language is really like. Mr. Poe should have written in Yiddish and he would have been memorable forever —you understand?"

The tall man is memorable. His name is forgotten. His eyes are always before me, with the potatoes and Poe. His voice, half gone, yet thrusting, had a holding quality; much as if he had changed his place with Poe seventy-five years earlier. Everything was being transformed on Hester Street, where Poe may never have walked, but he had lived long enough in various areas of New York to know some earlier peddlers. I called the old man Old Mr. Poe and he was that, with his bushels, potatoes and his Biblical beard.

A workingman's literature by a self-created intelligentsia, homespun, Old World and New World, was in being. The peddler, self-employed on two wheels, a millionaire of no standing and standards—a man rich in potatoes and beets, who traveled about with his pushcart, or with a large basket, or a pack, and saw everything, especially the harsh-stained ghettos—was as much the creator as the subject. He was only too real for all sorts of our Poes and Whitmans. His image was all-embracing and total . . . and my father, whenever he talked about poetry, which was rare indeed, would mention men like Morris Rosenfeld. Rosenfeld had written "I am a Millionaire of Tears" as well as a poem called "My Little Boy," which we all knew as children. But Rosenfeld was not a peddler, said my father—he was an intellectual and a former Yeshiva student. The Yiddish poets of

133

my father's day wrote lyrically and intensely. Others did a form
of lyrical broadside, socially denunciatory, in advance of Carl
Sandburg and Edgar Lee Masters or poets like Arturo Giovan-
nitti, the Italian trade unionist leader and radical. It was a time
of social quickening, with anarchists walking about America or
riding the freights, of hoboes who were revolutionaries testing
the new industrialization's soul in its relationship to man.

The greatest Jewish poet, said my father, was Yehoash, or
Solomon Bloomgarden, also not a peddler. He was among many
who were changing their names back to the Hebrew, giving up
their German-cum-Nothing adopted names. Poets? They came
as the gifted immigrants to our ghettos, as mystical doctors for
our sad souls. There was Abraham Raisin, who had come to New
York in 1908 from Russia and wrote a very direct folksong type
of Yiddish poetry. It was a time of no names and names; of
quarrels between Abraham Cahan, of *The Forward*, and others;
for Cahan insisted on attempting to use Yiddish as a language
of its own, purified of other languages. But Cahan's position
was like that of Mustafa Kemal Pasha, trying to remove Arabic
from Turkish, some years later . . . and with the peddlers, if not
with the poets, everyone held onto the accents from other lands.
It added more than the prosaic to the tastes of the multiple
tongues of the Lower East Side.

There were peddlers who talked their special kind of poetry,
in sarcastic shorthand; a verbiage built upon sentiment, nonsense—and their profession of peddling. A peddler, Tasrak, who
arrived in New York in 1889, wrote Yiddish sketches with very
witty backgrounds—thereby achieving more recognition than
he had gotten as a peddler of *tsimmes*.

One day I went to see Old Mr. Poe, the potato man on Hester
Street. I knew, with all the sliding accents, every sound of Poe's
"The Valley of Unrest." It was the way we memorized poetry—
and some learned, dutifully, to hate it. It was a drill in memory,
if not in meaning. What could I have known about the interior
of the poem? It was a poem to be learned by rote, recited by

134

sound, slid over when the reading was hard, made to sound mystical when it was simply rhythmical. Furious, all too curious, lost or found in sounds that were awesome, I was between potatoes, onions, beets, carrots, and fat women holding onto bags made of oilcloth. The women were stuffing vegetables into their bags . . . and I, cocky, over five cents' worth of potatoes, was reciting to Mr. Old Poe, the Peddler:

> *Once* it smiled a silent dell
> Where the people did not dwell;
> They had gone unto the wars,
> Trusting to the mild-eyed stars,
> Nightly, from their azure towers,
> To keep the watch above the flowers,
> In the midst of which all day
> The red sun-light lazily lay.
> *Now* each visitor shall confess
> The sad valley's restlessness.
> Nothing there is motionless—
> Nothing save the airs that brood
> Over the magic solitude.

One woman, thin, angry, gave me a shove. What did beets have to do with what I was saying to Mr. Old Poe? What nonsense was I reciting? Where was my mother? Where did I live? I lived on Cherry Street; maybe the real old Poe had lived there seventy-five years earlier, I said. Who was real old Poe? Real old Poe was a poet from an older New York—very famous. He had written . . . and I was about to talk about ravens and crows, but I was shut up, told to run home, wipe my behind, wipe my nose—and stop bothering the peddler. "Go away! He's a very busy man. Tomorrow is a *yontev—gedenk?*"

Another Jewish holiday . . . but I recited the poem again. Mr. Poe, new vintage, was listening this time—and before I knew it he was translating "The Valley of Unrest" into Yiddish. At that point the thin woman decided that both of us were

135

meshuga, and no longer wanted to buy his cheaper vegetables. Off she walked, putting her beets back and getting her nickel returned, with anger.

The tall old man stopped selling everything. He repeated his translation. It was almost literal, as I followed it with my Yiddish. Then he added, like a critic, "What does this poem mean to you, or the part that you've recited to me?" he asked.

I said, going from right to left foot, inching away, picking up potatoes and dropping them again. I looked down the street. I looked up at the sky. I watched the thin woman walking off, cursing our poetic session. And I said, painfully, "It means a place not like this—not Hester Street. No bargains in potatoes. . . ."

"What kind of place not like this?" asked Mr. Old Poe.

"It is a valley and there's nobody in the valley," I said.

"Not even God?" he asked.

I said, "Maybe God. Maybe wind. Maybe flowers, but not Hester Street or people."

"God is everywhere where people are, especially on Hester Street. In the wind, flowers, the potatoes you keep dropping, and in the woman who pushed you. Now, what does the poem you've learned mean? Have you understood it?"

Had anybody but the real Mr. Poe seventy-five years ago? At age eight it was difficult to understand the real Poe. It was music, sounds, words—and lost things I could not make out.

"Have you heard of the English poet, Thomas Hood?" he asked.

"No. Who is Thomas Hood?"

Mr. Old Poe, the potato man, said, "Listen to me just a little bit. It is called 'I Remember, I Remember.' But let me say it in Yiddish. The English, somehow, even though it was written in English, does not seem to have the *tam.* So listen, little boy."

> Ikh gedenk, ikh gedenk,
> Di hoyz vu ikh bin geven geboyrn,
> Di kleyne fenster vu di zun

136

THE TIME THAT WAS THEN

Hot areyngekrokhn in frimorgn;
Er hot keynmol gekumen tsu fri,
Nur gebrakht tsu lang a tog,
Ober itst—vintsh ikh oft az di nakht
Hot meyn otem avekgetrugn!

His accent was not mine. It sounded more Hungarian-Yiddish than Russian-Yiddish. But I had not told him that I knew the Hood poem as I translated his rendering back into English much as Hood, an Englishman, and hardly from Hester Street, had written it:

I remember, I remember,
The house where I was born,
The little window where the sun
Came creeping in at morn;
He never came a wink too soon,
Nor brought too long a day,
But now, I often wish the night
Had borne my breath away!

Now it was the way Thomas Hood wrote it, if not in a peddler's Yiddish . . . and Mr. Old Poe, amid his vegetables, heard me repeat his Yiddish, sound for sound, in English, but not image for image.

I was right, I knew. He was off . . . but he was saying, "Little boy, this is not a good translation, I know. But around old women and bargainers—what can I do? Come back tomorrow and remember another poem—and maybe we'll both do better. So run home now, *boychik*. No Mrs. Yenta tomorrow—yes? We'll have some poetry *anuye*. You are a real *dinchazzen*"—a word I did not understand. But my father, when I repeated it, said it meant "to study" or "to learn by heart."

The peddler and his potatoes and Mr. Hood and the real old Mr. Poe were just part of the odd literary Lower East Side. In

137

dozens of newspapers, weekly and monthly magazines, all the Yiddish poets were writing. They had their idioms, accents, new and old themes, lyrics that were savage or too tender, peddling their books to friends and enemies, purifying a speech that had suddenly come of age. English, with the generations that followed, was to take on some of the Yiddish flavors of another time . . . and then English was to do for us what Yiddish had done for our fathers, mothers and relatives.

The culture-in-making had produced poets like Yehoash—he died in New York in 1927—who, with some normal ambivalence, could say: "Do not sing! Curse! Curse!" In a poem, not adequately translated, he does:

> Sweetly blows the breeze of spring
> Every twig in green attire.
> But in my breast there molders
> The curse I seek to silence . . .

Morris Rosenfeld, the ghetto poet my father had told us about, also died in 1927. Once a sweatshop worker, acclaimed as a poet, translated into a dozen European languages, he was the Yiddish poet most revered by us. The ghetto's shops and pushcarts were his natural habitat. His anger, energy, lyricism and proletarian sentiments are difficult to render into English, and rather than despoil Rosenfeld's Yiddish poetry I will not quote him in any of the many awkward translations made into English.

Much earlier there had been Naphtali Hertz Imber, writer of the Jewish national anthem, "Ha-Tikvah," who died in New York in 1909. Zangwill used Imber as a character in his novel *Children of the Ghetto*—immortalizing him as Melchizedek Pinhas. In "Ha-Tikvah" he sings:

> Hear ye, brothers, in the land of your wanderings
> The voice of one of our seers;
> That only with the last Jew will our hope perish.

138

There were, when I grew up, many poets whom I knew well, poets like I. Manger, Mani Leib, Yosl Cohen, and I think of the many I met later, to have a drink—often tea, often whiskey, coffee, seltzer water, celery tonic—and back to the whiskey again; poets named and not named; an alphabet of names that cannot be listed because there were so many. They are forgotten, half-remembered, recalled for some lyric, a joke, a bargain in a book, a political discussion.

Who had not been a peddler? There was Benjamin Schlesinger, one of the earliest leaders of the ILGWU—who had sold matches way back in 1892—one of the great leaders at the founding of the union and through its later battles. If peddling did not always turn a man into a poet, it made some tough union leaders, and wealthy merchants—as soon as they got rid of their carts.

I remember another peddler, not too far away from Mr. Old Poe. He was a real poet, who scribbled on bits of paper, gave away the paper, kept some of the better poems, and declaimed over his pushcart filled with fruit something that has bolted from my memory in its precise form—but went almost in this fashion:

> Potatoes come from where potatoes come from.
> Apples are not the same—they fall and rot.
> Tomatoes are love apples, but who loves anything here?
> Beets are red inside—a skin to hide their bleeding.
> Oranges, lemons, melons, figs, raisins—God!

There was also Philip M. Raskin, an old friend, hardly a peddler, who died while I was in New Guinea during World War Two. Many a glass of tea was drunk while poetry, in Yiddish and in English, talked to the two of us in its many tongues . . . and Raskin, sentimentalist, who had gone in his poetry from Yiddish to English—a language that was, in poetry, not his total essence—once wrote, so many years ago, a poem called "The Peddler's Case." For a juxtaposition, now far from Hester Street, I quote another sort of peddler's promises:

HARRY ROSKOLENKO

And then I look at my soul with disgust,
And am ashamed of its face.
A soul should have a decent store—
Not carry a peddler's case . . .

Poets came like the seasons—some were wetter, from drinking in the snow and the rain. My friend Chaim, peddler-poet, drank up what he sold on Hester Street—vodka for his galloping soul. He was Russian-Jewish, and when he got *shikered*, he would do Russian dances. Up! Down! Sideways! His kazatzka would have gotten him into the Don Cossacks—as a drunken dancer. He was the first example of a Yiddish poet who was also a drunkard . . . and there were tears, later, when he fought with his wife. And he had many—four at least—who tore at his hair when he was drunk; who ripped off his clothes, when he was sober; who made scenes at his pushcart, when he was writing poetry. But since he had never bothered to marry any of them, he left them, moved his pushcart to another street, continued his drinking, his poetry, his dancing—and found another "wife." Oddly, despite all of the hair-pulling, he had a massive growth of gray hair in his middle seventies—and was healthier than two young colts running in the rainy grass.

Chapter 9
The Yiddish Theater

The Yiddish theater's history is short, oblique, and a tale of many wandering Jews. Begun in the latter part of the nineteenth century, stemming from Poland, Lithuania, Romania, Russia, Austria, and Hungary, today, in 1971, this theater has gone through its major dramatists, its faultless actors, and its wandering audiences. Unable to renew itself, deprived of the continuity of the Yiddish culture that sustained it from the turn of the century until the 1940s, it has, literally, died in its amazing working clothes. The richer sons and daughters of the fathers and mothers who made up its Yiddish-speaking audience have not followed the cultural ways of their immigrant parents. The Yiddish theater is dead—*geshtorbn*. Time, radio, TV—and the English language—built its coffin.

During Biblical times the theater was forbidden by religious edict. So were sculpture and painting, for the restrictions about art were total. Later the Purim plays were allowed in the synagogues but only as religious festivals. God and belief were all that a man needed for his tokens of art; and play-acting was a form of spiritual idolization. But, despite 3,000 years of religious prohibition, art and the Yiddish theater stormed into the

141

more flexible nineteenth and twentieth centuries. It came along with all of the racially engulfing conflicts, the repeating pogroms, the vast immigrations. A new moral dispensation shunted aside the past religious taboos and the emerging theater created an aesthetic revolution. Various schools of acting were adapted, and within a quarter of a century a universal Yiddish drama was born—with great plays, unique acting styles, extraordinary actors, and distinguished sets. It was a theater, in Yiddish, mannered for a Yiddish culture, with socialist, orthodox, and bourgeois ladies and gentlemen very much at home on Second Avenue.

My communion with the early Yiddish theater, as an occasional being-taken-to spectator, runs from 1913. Then, aged six, I had seen some musical comedies and serious, mysterious plays. But the unique years came later—between the wallowing-in-plenty of the 1920s and the aftermath, the poverty and crises of the 1930s—when I, like my Marxist friends, was changing the world, including the Yiddish and American theater.

The Yiddish theater, prior to the arrival in 1891 of Jacob Gordin as a playwright, performed trash—*shund*. Gordin, born in 1853 in the Ukraine, knew the world of the *Hasid*. His father had been a *maskil*, an enlightener, and the inheritance that Jacob Gordin, a handsome, aristocratic, overly pained Jew, got from his father made him a demonic creator as an educator-playwright. His nature, often too severely dedicated, brought on feuds and conflicts—not always of his own distillation. His most egotistical feud was with Abraham Cahan of *The Forward* . . . yet Gordin could write a letter to a friend, saying: ''Every playwright, willingly or unwillingly, must adapt himself to the abilities and shortcomings of the leading actors. . . . On the other hand, the playwright faces an audience part of which wants realism, another romanticism, and a third just a bit of burlesque. . . .'' Gordin was being very kind.

When Gordin arrived the Yiddish theater played loud *gezenge*, *marshe*, and *tentze*—songs, marches, and dances—influenced by American and German productions. Nor was that novel in New York, whether done in Yiddish, German, or Russian. It arose

142

out of the new immigrant's compulsion to act as American as
the next foreigner. With a mass Yiddish-speaking population
centered in New York, Gordin, the educator, was reaching for
a theater of enlightenment—to prepare his people for the mixed
moral, social, and political changes about to embrace an old people in the New World. What was old was the ancient pains . . .
and New York had tomorrow's illusions.

In 1891 there were actors—imposing people who had migrated
earlier. Gordin met Bertha Kalish, Jacob Adler, David Kessler,
Boris Thomashefsky—the elite of the Yiddish stage, who, said
my father, used to orate, center stage, as chosen brethren of a
theater trying to conquer the end of the old century. But Gordin
transformed the elocutionists into something more, with his extraordinary plays, his directional skills, and his insistence that
actors act, not just talk in compellingly beautiful voices and
gestures.

Gordin wrote one of his most distinguished plays, *Mirele Efros*,
before the end of the wallowing century. When it was done in
1898, the critic, B. Gorin, wrote the following: "*Mirele Efros*
marks a new effort in Gordin's creativeness. Its basis is the same
as that of his *Jewish King Lear*. The subject of both is adapted
from Shakespeare's famous tragedy. But *Mirele Efros* is a big
leap from *Lear*. In *Lear*, the playwright is afraid to take a step
of his own, and keeps onto Shakespeare's coattail. But in *Mirele
Efros*, Gordin stands firmly on his own feet. The plot and the
characters have nothing in common with Shakespeare's tragedy,
and the play is entirely his own. Gordin has found his way in
Mirele Efros."

Seventy-two years later, the self-exiling Polish-Jewish actress
Ida Kaminska was to bring her theater to the United States to
put on Gordin's play, the adapted *Lear*—with contemporary
Jewish problems.

Though *Mirele Efros* became a classic, other plays of Gordin's
infuriated Abraham Cahan, especially the play *The Purity of
the Family* . . . and the feud between the two men matured.

Gordin, a socialist on his own merits, loathed cheapness,

143

money-grubbers and their involvements. Cahan, the official socialist, the sacred protector of unions, found fault with anybody who attacked trade unions—even those that might have corrupt officials. An earlier play by Gordin, *The Russian Jew in America*, done in 1895, had satirized a corrupt union official named Hudsak . . . and the feud began. It would end only when Gordin died in 1909—and Cahan would write, years after Gordin's death: "The stage is a key to the gates of popularity. And because Gordin was the center of the stage, he became popular and important. People sought his acquaintance. He was surrounded by the intelligentsia. . . . In the beginning, we were friendly. . . . His pride and explosive sensitivity created for him some personal enemies, but he had many admirers. . . ."

Earlier, aware of the nature of opportunism—and its effect on some socialists, union leaders, and the suddenly wealthy—Gordin had written: "The race of radicals for money and career is the cause of the vulgarization of socialism and art, and consequently leads to the victory of the parvenu in elections and in the theater. . . ."

My first visit to a Yiddish theater as a cultural addict, age six, took place when my Orthodox father took me to the bulging National Theatre on Houston Street and Second Avenue. It was a cold Sunday afternoon. There was, sharing in the basic confrontation of art, a burlesque theater in the same building, with photographs of half-dressed girls at the left side of the entrance. On the right was what we came to see. My father, very *frum*— religious—averted his eyes, staring at the right. I looked left but I did not know what I was seeing—then. Soon we were crowding up an elevator to the top floor. Old women in shawls, older men in fur hats and coats, red-cheeked girls, and young boys in *yarmulkes*. What an audience for *shund*!

What were we going to see? I did not know, nor did my father. It had something to do with dancing, he said; not a play—but *gezenge* and *tentze*. The girls, when done with their burlesque, left one floor and went to another. They divided their animations between Yiddish *shund* and an early version of American strip-

144

teasing, doing erotic-minded dancing for both mid-cultures-in-
the-making at the National Theatre.

My father had been sold the two tickets by his sick-and-death-
benefit society for their yearly benefit for the living and the
dead. We were the living, watching the *shikses* dance and prance.
Jewish girls did not do what we were seeing, said my father.
They were showing this and that; derrières, a bit of tit, all of
their thighs—and my father was becoming all the more religious.
He turned his face away. Young boys, most of them embarrassed,
were doing likewise by fatherly direction. My father, on hearing
the words of a song the dedicated prancers were singing, soon
put his hands over my ears. It was an afternoon in Yiddish
Puritanism. One of the songs that escaped his hands went like
this, in mannered Yiddish:

> In der Toyre steyt geshribn
> Mit a shikse tor me nisht lign—
> Oy—der bester srore oyf der velt!

Which meant, not literally translated:

> In the Torah it is written
> With a shikse you cannot sleep,
> Oh, the best piece in the world!

The Second Avenue theaters ran from Houston Street up to
Fourteenth Street—fourteen wide streets of cafés, coffeehouses,
theaters by the dreamer's dozen, all Yiddish; a few movie
houses, like Loew's; then vegetarian restaurants, first-floor tea-
rooms, first-floor parlors for chess or pinochle; everything mixing
in with coffee, vegetables, dairy, and the toxic European cuisine
available on the Avenue. It was a geography of burgeoning
values and sadder events. There were brutal strikes in New York,
pogroms in Russia—and the theaters reacted. There was the
permanent pogrom, with the Kishinev pogrom of 1903 worked
into some serious playwright's drama as the classical tragedy.
The pogroms were to herald the 1905 revolution after the Rus-

HARRY ROSKOLENKO

sian-Japanese war; with some Russians, defeated, evaluating
their Slavic soul while killing some Jews.

There were plays about cossacks, with whips, and life in the
shtetl—the village. There were plays about immigrants—the
greenhorns just arrived. There were exalting, tearful dramas
about children, just orphaned; about a patient wife, finally joining her husband in New York, to discover that he had either
taken another wife or at least an impatient mistress. The plays,
the dramas, the tears, the harsh laughter, involved divorces—
gets; sweatshops; the Jewish boss—and, of course, the Jewish
workers getting revenge. There were plays within plays, with an
enormous amount of involved Yiddish philosophy. It was metaphysics and Yiddish mysticism, with both triumphing over
reality in the last act—with Judaic probing of the wandering
soul.

The real heart of the Yiddish theater was religious ritual and
the inevitable relationship between the dramatist, the viewer,
and God. This theater had begun as early as the ninth century
—at the Purim plays in the synagogues. But in my father's time
one could not walk about the Lower East Side or on Second
Avenue without seeing the exterior influence of the Progressive
Dramatic Club—an offshoot of the far-reaching Goldfaden
Movement. Started in Europe, this movement was transplanted,
without actors or scenery, to our tumultuous streets. As an earlier
arrival, Abraham Goldfaden, poet, playwright, and missionary-
dramatist—the moral founder of the Yiddish theater—had set
the stage for Jacob Gordin. In 1905, at a dinner honoring him,
Goldfaden said, "This branch of culture has been neglected
by the Jewish people. Seeking theater among other folk, I became a devotee of drama. I decided to write a play in Yiddish
. . . something new. The Jews had no actors, there was not even
a play available. . . . I sought out youths, choir singers, I rehearsed. . . ."

And others rehearsed as well. The ghetto was transforming
itself into a theatrical Holy Land. The Progressive Dramatic
Club began in New York in 1902, its purpose: "to develop a

146

public for the theatre and a theatre for the public. It was a guiding light in the struggle for a better Yiddish theatre.''

Begun in a stinking basement on East Broadway, with my father attending some of the plays they did, when they did not offend his orthodoxy, the Progressive Dramatic Club soon had its own audience just as the German Theatre in Greenwich Village did, and the later Provincetown Playhouse, where Eugene O'Neill's early works were produced. A Yiddish theater, ready to do baffling plays by Yiddish and European dramatists, had begun in the lowest emptiness of Manhattan, close enough to where the original island had been bought—by a minor migration, for much less than heart and God.

The Yiddish theater depended on the assorted critics in the Yiddish newspapers and journals—the café intellectuals. A review by a well-known poet, turned critic, meant that he liked the poetry in the play; a review by an actor, out of work, that he liked one of the women. A review by a real critic dealt with the solidity of the play and some of the actors; one by an editor was likely to discuss all interrelationships. For the entire Yiddish press, with an ego as large as the ghetto, and God, was most demanding politically and spiritually. Art, to many, had a spiritual heart somewhere. What was the playwright's intent? How much of the Torah and the Talmud was in the drama? What sort of Jew was the leading character? Where was God in the play? Where was man? Was this country different? And there was the old country, as well—and memory.

But what reached the critic's eye as high seriousness was, usually, the moral philosophy behind the play—not the *shund* dancing and the theatrics, or the clang and the purring of a Second Avenue operetta ringing away, financially, at the cash register. That was in a class by itself; fairly low, far away from Broadway in musical scores and choreography. The dancing dolls, too, were much too fat. But there was dancing in the serious dramas as well, as in Jacob Gordin's *God, Man, and the Devil*, and in *The Dybbuk*, by Ansky . . . highly stylized acting-dancing to purge the spirit.

147

HARRY ROSKOLENKO

It was Second Avenue's world of God and man, with the Yiddish press debating everything staged, whether good amateur or bad professional. Debate was inherent in the men who did the reviewing—a play, dismissed by six critics, had six others rivaling those with their acclaim. For over his sewing machine and his glass of tea almost everybody was a natural critic—discussion of a recent drama was an extension of merely sitting elsewhere and talking about the verities of Jewish humanity. One short session at a bench in Seward Park, over poppy seeds, and a few literary and drama critics, the pygmies of yesterday, became the giants of tomorrow. But the reverse was just as possible the day after.

None of the critics was extravagantly polite in his comments. Abraham Cahan, who often chose to write reviews for *The Forward*, and was an apostle of Yiddishism, could be socialistically savage when a play offended one of his many chosen and related values. On attending the opening night of Gordin's play *The Russian Jew in America*, Cahan angrily shouted from his seat at something allegedly offensive: "It's a lie!" Earlier, Gordin had lambasted Cahan's first novel, *Yekel*. Their public feud over art and ideas had a full head of Yiddish steam, with Cahan, for one year, writing some piquant attacks on Gordin as a thinker and a playwright.

The personal eye involved me, for I read all the newsstand's papers. I sold more of Cahan's papers, with his editorials, articles, play reviews, than any others—and since *The Forward* had more readers, it also meant more cash for my family. My father, using Cahan as his overall mentor—after the fleshier experience at the National Theatre—soon bought his own tickets, but not for song-dance entertainments. He preferred Gorki, he said . . . and Ossip Dymov's *The Awakening of a People*. In his halting, later years, when I could take him, he was to see a few plays done by Maurice Schwartz at the Irving Place Theatre—Dymov's *Hear, O Israel* and Jacob Gordin's *Jewish King Lear*. My mother, lost between *trern* and *lakhn*, preferred tears, Yiddish style,

148

about wandering orphans, and the heavy heart of Second Avenue's more turgid dramas.

Clubs and leagues, leagues and clubs—all progressive—sponsored advanced drama in lofts, cellars, stoop floors, and occasionally in real halls. The Progressive Club had a warm theater on Orchard Street that could seat 400. The Hebrew Dramatic League had a cold loft that seated very few. The Educational Alliance, to which I belonged, had all sorts of rooms for various types of audiences—as well as an auditorium, for the moral, meaningful, talked-about Yiddish plays. But the size and shape of the hall or room hardly mattered. What mattered was the play, the direction, the acting—and the competitive soul on stage, acting to an engaging audience learning its own spiritual and physical history, as a people.

The Yiddish theater, in the beginning, was an esoteric madhouse, as drama clubs merged and submerged, divided and united, splitting up by qualitative divorce and then uniting once again by the laws of economic as well as aesthetic determinism. And the way the contemporary Yiddish theater sprang up was the way it would end—just disappearing, like a pilgrim at the gates of heaven greeting the caretaker in English. As Second Avenue went from *kreplakh* to pizza, the inner and outer changes had, by then, pillaged the area of wonderful theaters and cafés. It was to turn into a shoddy avenue of hippies, nohopers, moral cripples, barbarians trying on grandfather's beard; and Yiddish, as a poet's tongue, was no longer a language for anything.

What plays did I see in those days as a boy? Who were the actors? How were the plays performed? What about the sets, the audiences, the prices?

The mobbing audiences came from the Jewish trade unions, from *vereins*, from sick-and-death-benefit societies and benevolent organizations. Every Jewish worker belonged to some society related to his old home in Europe, and they made up the majority of the audiences. They did not come with popcorn. They brought Turkish halvah, Jewish bagels, farmer cheese—sandwiched into a newspaper; American fruit, Russian candy, something to drink, and they carried on, equal in ego, as if they were the actors. Too often one could not hear the real actors, who were drowned out by the frightening comments, the extraterritorial noise, the public and private deep critiques, and then the overdone applause. The Yiddish theater of those days resembled the early English theater with its hurrahs, gusto, and lampooning. The only element lacking was Anglo-Saxon accents.

The prices were fifty cents, a dollar—and not much *up*; *up* just meant seats for two or three dollars. The sets, always applauded, were overpowering. You felt the mystical scenery merge with the actors, especially in the awesome play *The Dybbuk*. Ansky, the author, explaining it, said that *The Dybbuk* "is a realistic play about mystic people." The actors, no matter who played it, were consumed by their relationship to the worlds of the spirit and reality. After *The Dybbuk*, the other plays that I saw, including Jacob Gordin's *Kreutzer Sonata*, Gorki's *The Lower Depths*, Sholom Aleichem's *Tevye, the Dairyman*, could not reach the mystical and Judaic intensity of *The Dybbuk*. My father had paid a dollar then and I was transformed by Yiddish art.

Later I would see plays like Sholom Aleichem's *It's Hard to Be a Jew* or Peretz Hirshbein's *The Blacksmith's Daughter*. There were *Moishe the Fiddler* by Joseph Tcherniavsky and Oscar Wilde's *An Ideal Husband*—most of them done by Maurice Schwartz at the Irving Place Theatre, a burlesque house shifting between Yiddish drama and *goyishe* eroticism.

The young Jewish actors, waiting, always bearded, were anxious to play the major role in *Shylock*; but all of them could have acted any sort of part in a play called *A School for Envy*. For the envy between them was total; the jealousy over roles permanent. Their difficulty—the young Yiddish star being held back by an older star. Paul Muni was to experience that for years as Muni Weisenfreund, an Austrian Jew, whose parents were actors . . . and Paul Muni, in Maurice Schwartz's Yiddish Art

150

Theatre, was to play stated seasonal roles in Peretz Hirshbein's *The Blacksmith's Daughter* and in Sholom Aleichem's *It's Hard to Be a Jew*. But at the end of a season he would be dropped by Schwartz. Then out into the hinterlands of the Bronx went Muni, to do a season of operettas, marches, and dances—exiled there by Schwartz's towering envies. A year later Muni was back, full-bearded, playing alongside Schwartz—but never in roles that Schwartz preferred to keep for himself in his almost one-man theater, where no actor dared overshadow his substance. After ten years as a bearded elder in the Yiddish theater, Paul Muni arrived, full-blooded, as an American actor in Elmer Rice's *Counselor-at-Law*, on Broadway. Thereafter, he was to have many imposing Hollywood roles: *Zola, Louis Pasteur*, a Chinese in *The Good Earth*, a gangster, often, and *Juarez*. Bearded or shaved, his natural substance should have remained on Second Avenue, for when the fine actors went, the audiences also decamped.

It was a theater partially in transition; much as if Yiddish were merely a prep-school language for the American stage. Many stayed and many left—each depending on factors of age, speech qualities, English as his nonbasic speech, and ambition. Two who were schooled in the Yiddish theater, eventually left it; Menasha Skulnik and Jacob Ben-Ami, going thirty blocks up to Broadway. And there were so many others, especially the children of Jacob and Celia Adler—Stella and Luther—a family rivaling the Barrymores. The generations soon separated theatrical families, and the Yiddish theater lost itself as the sons and daughters of these families left one heritage, to become full American citizens of Hollywood.

But the three unusual men my parents preferred, men who made the Yiddish theater immense, were Boris Thomashefsky—the patron saint; David Kessler, second in the trinity; and Jacob Adler.

Before them, much earlier, there was hardly a theater—certainly not *directed* actors. With them came the playwrights of universal merit, assured of the stature of these actors. There

151

were Rudolph Schildkraut and his son Joseph, with Joseph eventually going to Eva Le Gallienne's Civic Repertory Theatre, to do an amazing *Liliom*. But before Rudolph left the Yiddish stage, Joseph was to lease the Bronx Art Theatre for his father, for one year—before Hollywood made its claims on father Rudolph. Between Rudolph's acting in Asch's *God of Vengeance* and Joseph's *Liliom* both are permanently remembered no matter what language they wove their beards, mustaches, and costumes in and about.

There was Bertha Kalish, the first to go American after being a great Yiddish tragedienne—about whom the critic, B. Gorin, would write: ". . . her leaving the Yiddish theatre, which robbed it of part of her repertoire, *Sappho* and *The Kreutzer Sonata*, was a portent of what would happen to the best strength of the Yiddish theatre which will be stolen away by the power of the American dollar."

There is no alphabetical guide to the Yiddish theater in New York, but it would run beyond the letter Z for its actors, playwrights, directors, and scenic designers. All of them created its short, elevating history. The actors played the major plays of the world; one night, Molière's *Don Juan*, the next Ibsen's *Ghosts*. Between Norwegian, English, and French classics, they played *Uriel Acosta* by Karl Gutzkov, *Man and His Shadow* by Z. Libin, *Love's Byways* by David Pinski, and hundreds of other plays written in Yiddish and performed by zealous men of amazing abilities—to deepen our understanding of more than the ghetto's self-enclosed provinces of the mind.

America knew of Jewish peddlers, businessmen, strikers, socialists, doctors, but Jewish actors—that was unbelievable! And with 250,000 Jews as a city-wide audience during my father's time, Saturday nights and Sunday afternoons were a ghetto spectacle inside and outside the theaters. Outside, greeting each other, were cousins and aunts. People kissed and people did not kiss. Somebody was *broyges*—angry. Who had not invited whom to a wedding? To a *bris*—the circumcision ritual? To a Bar Mitzvah? To a funeral? Who had *geshtorbn*? Who had gone to

Jerusalem? To the Bronx, Westchester, Boston, Chicago? And what took place outside, soon took place inside. Then the audience celebrated a *yontev*, a holiday, of acting, intellect, and the senses, all mingling togther, hardly separated by the stage, the greasepaint, the trying emotions of the actors. For, when the applause came, they were as one, with due deification for some star they were ennobling . . . and people who have heard David Kessler and Maurice Schwartz, with their natural speech, knew they had heard a David Garrick of their own.

For ego values, as well as for sharing in the managerial wealth, Yiddish actors had theaters named after them—following the English tradition. David Kessler, Boris Thomashefsky, and later Maurice Schwartz—with five boroughs of Jewish people following them to their self-named theaters . . . and in time I saw them all. My father liked David Kessler, and he said, once, over a hurried glass of schnapps, "He talks like a Litvak—so that's good enough—and he does serious plays. Others are fakers. Take——" And my mother intruded "You mean Jacob Adler? How can you say such a thing?"

"I did not say such a thing—not Adler. Certainly not Adler!"

"So who is the faker?"

"A man named Yosel Pisher—so there!"

"I never heard of him," went my mother.

"Nor have I!"

During the 1930s I was to meet many actors, especially from the ARTEV, the radical Yiddish theater. They wore red ties and had long hair, when they were not bald. They were loved by the girls, like poets, for their private mysticism. But the theater was one thing; the people in it, another kettle of hot water. My father, who loved the theater, would never have invited an actor into his home, for there was something not really kosher about them. They had a touch of the *goy* . . . and, years later, when I was a member of a propaganda group called Proletarian Laboratory, and the worst actor in the crusading group, my father thought I was really demented, and he said, "A poet, yes. A writer, yes. But not an actor—not an actor!"

153

HARRY ROSKOLENKO

The Yiddish theater had many founders, experimenters and conceits, but it was men like Benjamin Kramer, who had created the first 100-seat loft theater in New York, the Hebrew Dramatic League . . . the Jacob Gordins and the Goldfadens, who rid the theater of its musical pink cream cakes and *drek*—to give all sorts of Jews some of the black bread of real art.

It was to become a theater of many worlds, traveling wherever there was a Yiddish audience. A man spent his quarters and his kopeks as fantasy and reality became another mask within his world—universal, strange, cruel, gentle—Yiddish-Hebrew-Judaic. And it was Jacob Gordin, who had written forty-one plays in Yiddish, who, as early as 1908, with some prophetic vision wrote a play called *Demented America*—his final play; and when he died the next year, the Yiddish theater lost one of its baffling geniuses.

It was a Yiddish theater, with various accents. It was lyrical, intense, combative, experimental, commercial, noncommercial, all art, all-embracing, with a language that grew with each new play and actor. Yiddish was unique in its newness as a dramatic language, for all the senses were engaged endlessly. But it was to die within and without; a language without readers, writers and audiences. America was to engulf it by the time the Second World War came—when it should, with its extraordinary abilities, have created another theater from the horror and terror of the Nazi invasions and death camps. But it had been diluted much earlier by the singing—the kind that I had heard with my father so many years before at the National Theatre on Houston Street and Second Avenue . . . and my father blushed, turned his head away, turned my head away—and put his hands over my ears.

> In the Torah it is written
> With a shikse you cannot sleep,
> Oh, the best piece in the world!

Chapter 10
The Man with the Little Black Bag

When I was a small boy, many unusual doctors on the Lower East Side had their uncluttered, almost instrumentless offices on East Broadway, for a location on this street gave them more than mere medical status. East Broadway was a street of many professions, especially Yiddish journalism. East Broadway had other unique characteristics, for the *shnorring* offices of every Jewish charitable organization sat, cheek to pocketbook, over East Broadway like so many begging crows.

It was, with this bizarre accumulation, as professional as it was charitable for doctors to open their parlor-floor offices on a street that treated the body, the soul, the heart, the intellect— and everything that was tribally Jewish in my time.

From the doctors' one-stoop-up domains their eyes spanned Israel-in-the-making on East Broadway. For dozens of self-help institutions and schools teaching Hebrew, Jewish history, preparing students for the rabbinate, stood on East Broadway with exterior and interior commitments that would, in about forty years, help to realize what was then only an idea called Israel

HARRY ROSKOLENKO

. . . and the street needed everybody, especially the doctors with the little black bags.

The doctors were our giants, though they may not have resembled Solomon or David the King except in our imaginative associations. When the doctors left to make their sad rounds, we knew, as we watched, that we were in the presence of holy men. The little black bags, hanging slackly, added other dimensions of mystery to their glory, as they entered their small electric cars.

Literally everything they wore was black or gold. They were mustached and bearded. Their gray-black goatees marked them as doctors. They wore black suits, vested, with dangling gold chains; black glasses that they pinched on their noses; black hats, with the Homburg touch on top to make them most superior; starched shirts, the collars like so many professional emblems flying under their heavy chins. In the little black bags they carried stethoscopes, tongue depressors, thermometers, bottles of medicine—and their Old World smiles, not put into the black bag. The smile ranged about an East Broadway doctor's worried face—and that was our medicine.

Our ills were very simple in those days. Pimples, acne, youthful complaints, which, we were assured, we'd grow away from in a few years. Cancer, known and unknown, was another disease we'd heard about. But consumption or TB was the most dreaded disease—or so we heard from our parents. It was talked about like so many secrets, low-voiced, when we were asleep; or, when we suddenly woke up, to hear father or mother say, "Tante Anna has consumption. God must help her. We must help her. She has worked too hard . . . and we must take care of the children when she goes to the hospital in the country. . . ." Then came the man with the little black bag to verify what my mother had said early in the morning.

But whatever illness was about, there he was—his light-dark presence holier than the rabbi's; his faith in our faith made obvious by his ever-warming voice and smile. He took care of the lice my mother missed in her research into my head; or German

156

measles, chicken pox, and, of course, whooping cough—which sounded as if we were about to fly through the ceiling or burst through the window and jump over the fire escape, we coughed so dramatically. But with the doctor present, we knew that we were not about to die like cats and dogs.

When he arrived he was given a glass of tea from the samovar that was forever lit. A piece of lemon lay on a plate along with cubes of sugar. He put a sugar lump into his mouth and sipped the tea through it, Russian-Jewish style. He asked particular questions about every child—and he remembered who had had what, weeks ago, without any reference card to index his way toward our illness or health. He studied us, thumped a bit here and there, examined our chests, groins, armpits, ears, eyes, nose, throat—like a whole clinic of doctors. We were healthy, obviously; all but one of us, the one for whom the doctor had been called. One day it was my kid brother, then called Velvel, or William—he is now Bill—and he was put to bed, cough and all. He was given some brown syrup, patted on the head, warmed in bed, smiled at with Russian, Polish, German, and Yiddish words —and he was better the day after the next morning, ready to get sick again.

Another day it was I, the author, who had been out the night before selling newspapers that would not get sold in the rain. I was burdened with so many soaking editorials—and the papers had to be thrown away. I had a fever. I was given more of that brown medicine and hot tea. I was bathed with alcohol, dressed in heavy sweaters—and also put to bed. Two days later I was back with the newspapers or playing stickball with the fighting gangs on Cherry Street.

To keep a boy in bed, when so many street challenges were shouting up from the street, was useless—unless I was given a book to read. I was—a book my sister Edna got from the Chatham Square Library just off East Broadway. It was a novel by G. A. Henty, the Englishman, who made my youth all the more adventurous with his novels like *With Clive in India*; or Altscheller, an American, who fought the French and Indian Wars

157

in my bed. Henty, Altscheller, and the doctor made a boy well; but that was before sociologists, psychiatrists, and social workers came into our streets.

Medicine, and its practitioners, was an altogether different profession in my childhood from the profession and its practitioners today. The doctor's fee ranged from a quarter to fifty cents to a dollar per visit to the parlor floors on East Broadway. If the parents did not have the money, money was not asked for by the doctor; the doctor immediately understood. It was not actually charity. The husband was either out of work or on strike. It was temporary, too. Besides, the doctor had a kinship to the family he was visiting. He came from the same town, village or city. He was never called by his first name, but by his professional title, in tones of awe and obeisance.

The doctor's office had leather chairs and an oak table, with very little equipment visible. The equipment was in his hands and his head, said my mother. He had all sorts of broad sympathies and was immersed in all the major events of our lives. He had come over as an immigrant and we were the children of immigrants—almost as foreign as our parents despite our desperate ways of trying to alter that . . . and his office was filled with parents, children, conversations in every direction, children talking to children, parents to parents—and the doctor to everybody. The talk was about jobs, relatives, better apartments, hot water, bigger stoves in the kitchens, toilets in the apartments, not in the hall; bread, fish, milk and potatoes. It was all-inclusive, heated, loud when noise was necessary, or low when it was about somebody about to die. Once again TB . . . and you could see it in the pale wet faces of many of the children. Their eyes were glazed, dark, heightened in their frightened stare. They could not play games, run or fight. They sat in the parks huddling to the sunbeams. Somewhere, some hospital with X-ray machines, we were told, had found out that they had consumption.

There he was, the doctor in his black suit, taking us into his office—away from the mobs of the sick in the waiting room. Once inside you saw a skull or a skeleton—and that was enough to

158

make you better. It was put there, we thought, as a warning of what we would soon look like if we did not behave, in our mass fighting on the teeming, brutalized streets. The next hole in the head and we were skulls and skeletons, said the doctor. Stop fighting. Don't go with the gangs. Don't go swimming in the scummy waters of the East River. Go to Rutgers Swimming Pool. Don't play with dogs, cats, mice, birds—anything that crawled or flew. If you had an itch—don't scratch. There were an enormous number of ''do-nots'' and an equal number of what to do's. It was don't do and do do, in the end.

The doctor, who was not a lawyer, gave advice that sounded legalistic, political, social, religious, walking into many other professions as a kindly old man. He was also not a real-estate operator, but he advised us about what sort of apartment, or flat, to rent, when the next lease was up . . . one with more air, higher up—if we could manage to walk up six or seven tenement flights of stairs. He was a general practitioner and we were the recruits of his massive armies as we paraded from the waiting room to his office with the skull and the skeleton. We were the soldiers battling on the Lower East Side because it was so painful growing up, having nothing but parents, one cent in our knickers, fighting to get after-school jobs, to make that penny or that great nickel—and work, not fighting, was the doctor's final exhortation after every visit to his parlor-floor arena of broken heads and hands.

On his walls were his degrees—diplomas from medical schools in Moscow, Warsaw, Berlin, Kiev, and not from Columbia University. During my entire youth on the Lower East Side I do not recall ever seeing a degree from an American medical school. Further, the books in his glass cabinet and bookcases were seldom in English. They were in Russian, Polish, and German—and he spoke those languages, and more. His English was the kind our parents spoke, if less halting and less broken, though with similar accents. We, the children, were running away from these accents, to become native Americans in a hurry—and with the broken bones to show off our Americanization.

The process of becoming nonforeign, most American, had its

injurious concomitants when we played games. The handle of a busted broom was your bat. If you were on the losing side of a stickball game, the handle landed across your head—and the hole-in-the-head joke was developed in Yiddish culture. You did not need the hole, said the doctor. Nor the smashed fingers. Nor the belt to your guts. But the hole in the head was the most frequent ''accident'' when I was a boy. When the blood came down you went off to Gouverneur Hospital or to the doctor on East Broadway. A dirty handkerchief was your immediate bandage, put there in a hurry. The blood coming down got you into his office, away from all the talking patients. Once inside, with his slowness giving you another view of the skull and the skeleton, you were certain, then, that you were going to die. He nodded. Your father nodded. Your mother nodded. And then you nodded—and soon you were all bandaged, saved once again to become an older American boy.

There were other common injuries—like burns from the big bonfires we made on Election Day and on July 4, to celebrate the highest, biggest, patriotic fire on the East Side. There were the kicks that we got from the horses as we tried to get our soft rubber balls from under their hooves . . . or the bites from the mad dogs that made the East Side their juiciest biting fields. We were always reminded, after a bite—no more dogs. ''They are all mad and they belong to the *goyim*, besides.'' Rabies? All of the East Side's animals, we heard, had rabies. I expected to see kids foaming at the mouth. Every dog I saw snarled at me . . . and they bit. Therefore—no dogs, no rabies, no wandering around the *goyim* streets to play a dog's games.

Our doctor had a name—Nagorni. He had treated me for measles, whooping cough, pimples—whatever bothered a boy as a boy with too much running speed to and from fights. Dr. Nagorni was a heavily mustached man and he resembled the Kaiser, we thought, or the King of England—somebody most important to look at. All the Russian classics were in his office, said my father, in Russian. When I was eight, to move me from fighting to literature, he gave me my first personally owned, symbolic book, a wornout copy of *Crime and Punishment*, which I could

160

not read or understand for years after that. But whenever I came with my mother or father he would talk to them in Russian —which I then understood enough to understand that I understood what he was saying.

To get rid of my pimples, said Dr. Nagorni, I must get a woman—and he laughed. My mother blushed. My father thought that the doctor had gone mad or that he was an amoral scoundrel. What would a boy of eight do with a woman? Apparently I learned sooner than was necessary for my skin and my then small body. The doctor was most practical, somewhat Rabelaisian, totally a Russian, easily a great scholar—and he gave us all his wisdom and learning for fifty cents a visit.

Outside Dr. Nagorni's office was his small electric motorcar. It stood there like a totem pole overly shined by every kid on East Broadway. There were other cars, other doctors—and the cars of the politicians—but only Dr. Nagorni's car had that high shine in the summer sun. The car was loved as much as the doctor. It was watched over, with children and mothers cautioning other children and other mothers not to sit on it—just to dust it for the doctor's sudden departure. And there he was, tumbling down the stoop, puffing to his car, driving off at ten miles an hour down East Broadway. He would turn south at Montgomery Street and head toward Cherry Street, where I lived. He would turn left on Cherry Street, avoid trucks on their way to the Customs House, or horses carrying everything that horses still pulled in my time—and drive to Gouverneur Hospital. What he did at the hospital we knew well—the same thing that he did at his office on East Broadway.

He bandaged heads. He put splints on arms. He made some kid feel better and less bloodied with pain. From Friday afternoon to Sunday night was, despite the Sabbath, a long time to avoid fighting after you had made peace with God at the synagogue.

The medicines they gave us on East Broadway were almost homemade. The doctor had an enormous collection of colored bottles, each bottle labeled with large black letters. You read the bottle and you knew nothing. He read the bottle and he knew,

161

for he was mixing colors and smells . . . then the mixture went into a small bottle, which was given to your mother. The treatment was homely too, for our own mothers could make up many of the medicines. It came from folklore and old fishwives' tales. It came from Russia and Poland and the ghettos. There was always hot water for a stomachache; or lemon and salt for a sore throat; or various herbs, all smelling like China and India put together in the doctor's office. We never got prescriptions in Latin nor did we go to a drugstore. I never saw the inside of one when I was a boy.

The little man with the little black bag had a mythology built around his comings and goings. We knew where he went when he started out early in the morning—to the tenements. He climbed up five, six and seven flights of dank darkness. He roamed the railroad flats like a nurse from the Henry Street Settlement. He spent time in each flat with the sick and the nonsick. The talk was not always about pain, sickness, fear—though health was hard to get and to keep on our streets. The doctor was only being the all-wise medicine man even when he talked about union matters, or how to help a relative migrate from the Ukraine to Cherry Street, or whom to see and what to do after you saw someone.

He was our intellectual adviser, as well. At his office you would see all sorts of foreign papers, mostly socialistic. You got your medicine and your radical politics at the same visit—if there was time to talk. You heard strange names mentioned, and you never forgot them—names like Karl Marx, Tolstoy, Bakunin; anarchists, Bolsheviks, socialists, playwrights, novelists, freethinkers . . . they all went into the Russian words of the doctor; mystical names, the kind you would expect a doctor to use when giving you some medicine. But it was for the mind, not for the body; and off you went, all the more mystified at the sounds and who the owners of those names were and what they were doing.

The doctor was an all-embracing personage. He was God, at least. He was several angels, as well. He was bigger than the President, and that included George Washington and Abraham

162

Lincoln—whom we had to admire at school. But neither Washington nor Lincoln had brought us medicine, bandages, candy —nor could they stop the bleeding from a hole in the head. Therefore, the doctor was way up in the heavens of our far-seeking eyes. And he smiled much better than anybody we knew, wrinkled around his eyes and his forehead, to grace us in our savage ways as we grew up a bit every other day.

But it was, also, the things the doctor was not that enshrined him in our wayward affection. He was not anxious to get rich over our live or dead bodies. And if one of his patients died, he would go to the funeral like a member of the family—obviously even more of a man and a mourner than any of the dead man's relations. The patient could not have been saved. The illness had been TB, cancer, or heart disease—all the deadly things that only plagued, or so we thought, the old people. But there was the doctor at the funeral parlor, in the synagogue, at the cemetery, his eyes tearing. He was the man with the big white wings and just below the heavens in the synagogue.

The man with the little black bag, the dark suit, the vest, and the dangling gold chain is no more. He is part of another time just as we are part of another time's ways and pains. Another kind of humanity in another America made him, as well as the personalities and the needs of the immigrants. He personified the Hippocratic Oath—by his looks, his treatment, and his disinterest in payment. He was not on Park Avenue then, but on East Broadway. He kept us healthy at a time when pills did not become the total blueprint for the treatment of the whole or half of the boy.

He is no more just as the tenements are no more—the old tenements that existed before the automobiles and the wheels and the highways began to pollute us. The little man could not function today—unfortunately. His skills have only half gone to Park Avenue, to specialization, to group medicine, to greater illnesses, to national nervousness, to breakdowns that are cosmic —and he is not around to treat the children of a sick city that no longer makes it human to be a man with a little black bag.

163

Chapter 11
The Rebbe

The Rebbe was usually an old man who wheezed, coughed, sneezed in your face, and smoked broken cigarettes. He looked all dead except around his sparkling eyes. His hair was a mass of wool, when he was not all bald. His hat, which was black, made him appear even more pious, especially if he wore a *shtreimel*. The *shtreimel* was a round, big-brimmed black hat that made him appear even more pious than would an ordinary hat. He moved about in a long, untidy black coat, often of satin, and lined, or a *peltz*, a fur coat though the kind of fur that made up the inner holdings of the coat was vague. Nevertheless, it was a coat which the Rebbe filled up with Yiddish newspapers, torn letters from relatives in Russia, tattered books that he pulled out—to show his scholarship. The pockets—and it was a coat consisting more of pockets than coat—were his repositories for the day, for the week, for the year, for all of his peripatetic ways as a talker about God.

He came to our house in the afternoon after school had let out, as dinner was being cooked, as children were being washed, scolded, and harried, and he was always a witness to something sad, something not quite happy. If it was tragic, he was soon not the teacher. He was the able comforter over a glass of tea and a squeeze of lemon. He took his tea with a lump of sugar in his mouth, and he listened, nodded his head, much as if he were listening to a passage interpreting God's mysterious ways that late afternoon, or why Chaim—the youngest boy, who had come home from school with a bloody nose—had a bloody nose. What did the Talmud have to do with a bloody nose that wintry twilight, was the question.

He nodded all the more. Nodding was an affirmation, just like praying; the bent-over body, the mumbling voice, the incantations that made the synagogue like a mosque. We had some things in common with the Muslims: some prophets, our sense of God, some of our prayerful sounds and incantations—and Gan Eden, the future of the soul in Eden, as Semites.

The Rebbe was all things to his students; a tyrant made in the image of a spokesman of God. He was fat, thin, small, or bodiless. He had a beard, of course. His suit, or what passed for one, was always black. He stroked his beard in a Biblical fashion, much as if he expected another plague, on Egypt, to erupt from his beard. He had every other human habit of the Yiddish intellectuals: he picked his nose. When he blew his nose into a large handkerchief, it showed his learning. He was, also, a professional ear-picker, like his pupils.

When he called that afternoon with his pocketed books and lessons, I had just arrived from school—sufficiently harassed by my English teacher; and now another ordeal, in Hebrew, was about to begin.

No, I had not studied my lesson of yesterday. I had eaten apples and black bread and I had read H. G. Wells. What did Wells have to do with the Talmud? I did not know. I did not care—and I got the first slap, this one from my mother, who called me a fresh *yingatsh*—a young snotnose.

The Rebbe pulled at his beard. His left pinky picked at his left nostril. His right pinky dug into his right ear. Soon he was scratching his chest looking for a wandering louse. His hands went on and he scratched on. I watched, wondering why God was

166

not helping the Rebbe. Did God want the louse caught and killed?
Hardly. It was a living, crawling, bloodsucking thing—but part
of life. So was the Rebbe—part of my life and the cause of one
slap. When the second slap came my life was becoming painful
. . . and I sat up, no longer slouching, ready to participate in
another lesson . . . and I was saying, in Hebrew, following the
Rebbe's fingers on my book . . .

. . . Hear, O Israel: the Lord our God, the Lord is one . . .

I was queried about its meaning. The Lord is One, I repeated—not Two, not Three. This time the Rebbe slapped my
face, harder.

"The Lord is what?" I was asked in Hebrew.

I decided to repeat the whole line, and I said it proudly,
memorized, intoning like a cantor on the holy holidays: "Hear,
O Israel: the Lord our God, the Lord is One . . ." and I paused,
looked at my smiling mother, at the smiling Rebbe, who blessed
my head, stroked my face, beamed a bit, turned to another page
—and the lesson went on.

"Now, do you remember one day last month we had this section? Please read it *boychik*. . . ."

I looked. I stared. I glared. I had forgotten last month's lost
lesson. It was an entire thirty days away. I saw the Rebbe five
afternoons a week—and it was twenty lessons ago. How could
one, and a boy at that, remember a lesson about the Day of
Atonement?

I was atoning, soon enough—slapped into perdition. I remembered nothing, not one word, not one phrase—just that it had to
do with a special day that one starved on. To starve, however, was
hardly a way toward Hebrew scholarship, I thought. Then I said
it.

Why was it not—I was questioned by the Rebbe.

Because I would get weak, I said. I had to be strong, healthy,
the tough Jew able to win over the Gentiles who attacked me,
who called me a Christ-killer—I said proudly.

Is that the real reason I was asked—just that?

167

HARRY ROSKOLENKO

Yes. On the other hand it was good for the stomach, my mother had said—for she fasted one day a week . . . and I repeated what my mother had said to me often. It's healthy, then, Rebbe—not just weakening

Is that all you get from the Day of Atonement—I was suddenly asked.

I nodded sleepily. The air was bad. The stove was too hot. My friends outside, who did not have a Rebbe, were playing with the snow. Up went a snowball, missing a window.

My mother ran. Up went the window, out went her head, and she was shouting something in Yiddish, all of it very proper, nothing with a curse, all simple admonitions about windows, the cost of glass; that it was very cold with a broken window and the Sabbath coming . . . and out went the Rebbe's head, and he was yelling something in Yiddish that was not very nice. My mother pulled back, blushed, looked at the Rebbe and mentioned something to me about my father hearing about it—about the snowball, not what the Rebbe had said.

The Rebbe was back. The room was colder. I was nodding towards dreams of sleep or thinking of the downy comforter and the big pillows where I sank into heaven—when I slept.

Snowballs! They should be studying the Talmud, went the Rebbe. Bums! Future criminals! Cossacks! *Shlumperay*—and many other things, the Rebbe continued. He had lost the page. An entire lesson had been forgotten. The Day of Atonement was forgotten—briefly. For the Rebbe was turning, staring at one page, scratching a little bit. He was back at his nose where his greatest scholarship was. Then at his right ear—and now he had found a suitable page.

Did I, for instance, recall the following passage—taught to me two weeks ago?

I did, I said, and I repeated it softly.

Louder, *boychik*.

I was louder. I was intoning again, saying with even greater pride, from *Hallel*, the prayer said on the New Moon, on Passover, Pentecost, and Tabernacles, and on Hanukkah . . .

168

. . . Blessed art thou, O Lord our God, King of the universe, who hast sanctified us by thy commandments and hast commanded us to read *Hallel* . . .

My mother smiled. I sounded serious, sincere, lovable, religious, filled with grace and God. I had a soul, her eyes were saying to the Rebbe and to me.

Very good—but what was the next passage?

The Rebbe was being himself again. Yes, what? The Rebbe closed the book—and he wanted me to say it from memory.

It was, it was, it was, it was . . . and there was an awful lot of that—and silence. After these two words were repeated four times, I was stuck.

The next passage, please?

It is, it is, it is . . . and again silence.

Obviously there was a next passage or the Rebbe would not ask me. But what was it?

It was, it was, it was . . . silence.

It is, it is, it is . . . and silence.

The next passage—and the book was opening again. But the Rebbe's large hand was hiding the words on the page.

"Do you remember, *boychik*?"

It is, it was, it will be . . .

"*Nar*!" went the Rebbe.

So I was a fool—or just a boy with a bad memory, a new thing in my life.

"How will he ever get to the Bar Mitzvah?" asked my mother.

"I have six years to go. I'm only seven, Mama," I said, going back to my new language: *It was, it is, it will be* . . .

The Rebbe took away his right hand. There, unfolding, was the forgotten passage—and I was reading aloud again . . .

. . . Praise ye the Lord. Praise, O ye servants of the Lord, praise the name of the Lord. Let the name of the Lord be blessed from this time forth and for evermore. From the rising of the sun unto the going down thereof the Lord's name be praised. The

169

HARRY ROSKOLENKO

Lord is high above all nations, and His glory above the heavens. . . .

And I was suddenly blanked out again. Once more the Rebbe's right hand was playing his game of memory . . .

"And what goes next—after 'above the heavens'?" he asked with a challenge that was almost Biblical with dread.

I remembered—for I had seen the next few words. I recited, victoriously, slyly, watching my mother smile, happy that she had a son who was really going to be a learned one—*a galernter* . . . and I was saying . . .

. . . Who is like unto the Lord our God, that dwelleth so high; that looketh down so low upon the heavens and the earth . . .

And I stopped—the learned one was not learned any further. And the Rebbe was saying, "Yes, I know. A boy must stop for breath. So breathe faster, *boychik*. Tell me, what goes after 'the heavens and the earth'?"

Nothing, apparently. Not in my head, mind, or memory. I had seen the passage that stopped for me at "and the earth." I had gotten over the heavens to wallow back again to my *it is, it was, it will be* language of no learned distinction . . . and the Rebbe slapped me again.

My mother did the same and she called out, "*Nar!* Fool! What a learned one you are not!"

I was not something, by their affirmation. After all the wonderful words of praise to the Lord, I was somewhere below the cellar, deep in misery, aware that I must do something to alert my memory and keep their hands from slapping my face again.

It was a religious resolve—and I must study. At the age of seven, one had to show promises to the Lord, said my mother . . . to learn the ways of righteousness. And the Rebbe nodded, picked a nostril and an ear—and we went on again, to simple reading, not to memorizing lessons of another time.

The Rebbe was too old. Nose-picking would not make me a better student, said my father. Besides, I was growing up. I

170

should go to a *cheder*—a school for boys from three to ten—and later to the Talmud Torah, and spend three hours every afternoon, including all day Sunday, studying God's non-mysterious ways regarding the Jews.

Daily I would walk by a yeshiva—a college preparing students for the rabbinate. The Jacob Joseph Yeshiva was on Montgomery Street, four blocks from Cherry Street, and just around the corner from East Broadway. Could I go there? It was for real scholars, not for frightened students barely remembering their Hebrew lessons—and I was one of those. I was ready to become totally Americanized as soon as I could wear long pants, get a job, grow up to be about ten years of age, get rid of the sideburns and *peyess* that I had been, briefly, made to grow—and curl.

I saw the *melamdim*, the great teachers, dressed in long black coats and their wide black hats; bearded, bent, hungry, pale, dying—to make their students future rabbis. And the students were as old as I was—seven, eight, nine, ten; and the students, with their hats and *peyess* curling near their ears, were just as pale. No one had rosy cheeks—nobody but I, my brothers, my sisters, my mother, rosy-cheeked by heritage. I would, I realized, lose my health over the big Gemara books, or the commentaries of Rashi and Mishnah, the codified Oral Law. I would learn about agriculture, festivals, women, rituals, criminal and civil law—and matters of hygiene. But I was a clean boy, tutored or untutored, in and out of *cheder* and the yeshiva. I would be a good Jew—without rosy cheeks.

It was an old-young yeshiva. Whoever Jacob Joseph was, I did not know; but the foundation stone stated that the building had been laid in 1901. It was smaller than my public school, but just as gray, marbled, with a narrow entrance—to keep you in and not let you out easily. There were others, more memorable, like the Machzike Talmud Torah on East Broadway, built in 1886. There was a third one on Henry Street, past Clinton which looked even more scholarly, and there was the greatest of them all, the Yeshiva Isaac Elchanan, a school mentioned in awe, much as if it had been transported, brick by brick, from the ghettos of learned Jewish Poland. To advance Talmudic studies, it had been built, with great effort, in 1896. Obviously, if I was ever to become a *melamed*, any one of these schools would advance my mind and soul toward God's greater grace.

When my learned sister, Edna, then called by another name, much more Hebrew, went to *cheder*—and she was five years older—there were 307 *cheders* on the Lower East Side teaching 8,500 boys and only 360 girls. My sister, by those standards, was easily in the genius category—which I was not. She spoke fluent Hebrew, which I did not. She did her lessons, which I did not—with the old Rebbe, the one of the nose and the ears.

No yeshiva. It would be wasted on my head. A *cheder*, yes, said my adamant father. I was reading all the time, but not enough in Hebrew—in English; and the *cheder*, he thought, would change my drives enough so I would not end up as a *goy*.

All those *cheder-kheyders*. We pronounced it as we liked to. If you added a *k* it was still a school that you did not want to attend, not after the nine-to-three schedule at P.S. 31.

There were *cheders* for all sorts of Jews—Levantine, Sephardic, Ashkenazi, and I was one of those, I was told—an Ashkenazi, a Russian Jew. Our Yiddish and our Hebrew accents set us off from the others; therefore, I had to go to a *cheder* for the Ashkenazi—and I went, glancing at the Jacob Joseph Yeshiva every afternoon, as I walked, very slowly, to spend the hours between 3:30 and 6:00 P.M. at a dismal basement school on East Broadway. There, in some class or another, with kids that I had never seen before, I was soon arguing about all sorts of commentaries and resolving nothing. Yet it was an education to keep you a Jew; to give you pride in an ancient language; to learn codes, ethics, history—and all about the past heroism of my people at another time.

You learned, or you were slapped. No permission from parents was needed for slapping. It was expected, all too proper, and it had been done in Russia, Poland, Hungary—in all the ghettos of Eastern Europe. It went with learning faster, or

172

better—to accomplish what too often could never be done, in
New York. The city was too big. Too many other races and
nationalities and a heritage that set us apart—that did not melt
us into one huge glob of nationhood—were all over New York.
You learned what you wanted to learn, by rote, under stress,
while asleep, while rushing to the toilet, while rushing back—
with only two minutes given you to take care of your natural
functions. And back you were at the little table or desk. You
were sitting on a harsh bench. A small potbellied stove was behind you—preparing you to become, one day, a mature-enough
Jewish male.

There was much then that did not make you too happy, but
now, more than half a century since those slaps and bruised
knuckles, you love to recall what went on at the *cheder*. Somebody, a *melamed*, was up front. He was either too young or too
old. He was not American-born; it was too soon to develop
American-born Hebrew teachers. The lesson at the *cheder* was
an education on top of another . . . for there were English lessons
to be done that evening along with our Hebrew lessons; our pub-
lic-school studies running together with our *cheder* studies.
But galling homework was homework whether in English or in
Hebrew.

But there were *cheders* teaching more than *Khumesh* (Pentateuch). There was Zionism-in-the-making, and the Haskalah, or
the European Enlightenment Movement. All schools, when not
orthodox *cheders*, had other social, political, and religious
nuances behind them. There was the Love of Zion Movement, to
bring out a future Zionist—for migration to Palestine. There
was the Torah and Srorah school—learning and business—which
must have had some appeals in New York, especially with the
masses of immigrants ragpicking their way off the streets of
Manhattan—to learn, to earn, to become a *mentsh*, proper; to
be one's own and no longer a waif, awaiting the charity of
relatives to begin or to end. There was the school, too, which
concluded in the Talmudic stricture—"Respect the stranger
but suspect the stranger." And the Jews knew that too inti-

mately. The pogroms were not too far behind. They were strangers themselves—alien in a city of millions; sick, housed in tenements, the water tap in the yard, and the toilets there, too; strangers in a world of woe. They had a strange gift for comedy and it entered their language and their folklore.

We knew, too soon after the rabbis tried to make us good Jews, Yiddish words like *umglik*—tragic; *seykhl*—sense; *bobbe-myseh* —a tall story; *oysgematert*—tired out; *goneyvishe shtiklekh*— tricky doings. Our words were all too well related to our scholarship. We got the comedy and the tragedy easily mixed. There was *Az okh un vey*—tough luck; *gehakte tsores*—utter misery; *graubyon*—unmannered man; *mis*—ugly; *peygern zol er*—he should drop dead; and *balebatish*—respectable . . . and rarely indeed was such a word thrown at us.

It was like that in Yiddish. In Hebrew all was much more chosen, delicate, revered, holy—and nothing of an insulting nature was ever said to us in Hebrew. Our thoughts dealt with God—and Judaism. Hebrew concerned great tomes, worn away, and we were the children of those tomes. And the *melamed*, the *tsadek in peltz*, the man who was the scholar above all scholars, who wore a fur hat, a fur coat, who arbitrated between comments and commentaries—he was the esteemed judge of our world.

And the old rebbes used to come down our street, worn away by errant boys. And they brought with them the folklore and the ritual . . . and we took of both and became, years later, what we became in the United States.

Chapter 12
The Revolutionists

The revolutionists, in my gutter-school-*cheder*-newsboy childhood, came in all sorts of East Side relationships. How did one recognize a revolutionist? One didn't then; for there was nothing like wild hair and leather coats, their later gear. The signs were there, however, in their ways of thinking. I got to know a few through the kind of magazines and newspapers they bought from me. If a man asked for the *Jewish Morning Journal* he had few complaints of a revolutionary kind. When he bought radical journals like *Die Warheit*, or *The Big Stick*, then he was studying more bombastic journalistic methods for remaking the Lower East Side—or the whole City of New York. The would-be remakers from East Broadway were very explosive; others from cafés on Grand Street and Clinton Street were studiously quieter. It depended on where I walked. Some cafés were one flight up, where tea, seltzer, and schnapps were the revolutionary drinks; others were on the ground floor, where herring and potatoes helped a modest revolutionary dream about another future for the East Side's lowest men.

We knew, of course, about the great Emma Goldman, her lover Alexander Berkman, and the magazine, *Mother Earth*—

175

anarchist and literary. We knew of the Ferrer Center, a
school for anarchism. But, fortunately, I never met a man with
a bomb about to go off. Their bombs were on their tongues, in
their journals, in their café monologues. No one I knew had
ever tried to blow up any of the three bridges, or the ferry boats,
or the stockyards along Death Avenue, or Cherry Steet; nor the
police station, two blocks away from my home, on Madison
Street. They were men without bombs, writing pieces they kept
in their pockets for a month before testing them on an editor
for their literary mayhem.

Beards were normal then, well trimmed and proper. So were
long mustaches, bowler hats, canes, spats, and fur collars; for
even the most fiery man, ready to annihilate capitalism, was
medium neatly dressed; that is, all except Yankel, one of the
revolutionaries whom I knew well. He was a greasy bum. No
mustache. No hat. In the exact center of his bald head was a red
mark, apparently gotten from scratching his head about all the
revolutionary theories, if not their practices, that were being
talked about in my childhood. Yankel's penetrations brought on
a lot of falling dandruff, endless nose-picking, ear-picking, picking on his half-buttoned fly, lacing and unlacing his tattered
shoes, sneezing, spitting, coughing, wheezing, and going from
a cigarette to a cigar and back again. But through all this came
an enormosuly vituperative language. The bomb was definitely
amid the five teeth in his mouth. . . .

I remember Yankel because of his unusual rhetoric and learned
associations. Over a glass of tea, over a roll, which he dunked
into the glass, the sugar in his mouth, the cigar or cigarette tem-
porarily placed on the edge of the table, Yankel was mostly a
monologue. Yankel's usual companion was a cross-eyed taller
man, not quite disheveled, who had mats of hair, wore a large hat
that fell over his ears, and had an odd name—Charis. Charis
called himself an anarchist. Yankel called himself an anti-Marxist revolutionary; but neither of these words had any meaning
to me. They were, said my father, bad words for boys, men,
women—and politicians.

176

Yankel was shouting at Charis, who was quoting something from a piece of paper that he had pulled out of a stuffed pocket: "By association I mean a social order that shall take the place of the present township, to be composed of some hundreds or some thousands of persons, who shall be united together in interests and industry for the purpose of securing to each individual the following things: one, an elegant and commodious house; two, an education, complete and thorough; three, a secure subsistence; four, opportunity to labor; five, fair wages; six, agreeable social relations; seven, progress and knowledge and skill. As society is at present organized, these are the portions of a very small minority. But by association of capital and industry they might become the lot of all; inasmuch as association tends to economy in all departments, economy in land, fences, fuel, household labor, tools, education, medicine, legal advice, and commercial exchanges——" and Yankel broke through, saying, "What kind of crazy garbage is this, Charis?"

Yankel was back to his cigar, dropping ashes on his dirty pants, which had been a repository of everything since he had changed them last. "Madman! Anarchist meanderer! *Luft-mentsh*! Where did you copy all this stupidity?"

"From Fourier, *kleyne petzl*. Some learned scholar! It is utopianism, cooperation, collective living—something none of us do. . . ."

I was to remember Fourier's name—if not Charis's little document—but I was to look it up, years later, when I was arguing revolutionary theories. As a boy, however, it was all sound, combative and angry; argued daily on the minute by these merry merchants of revolution—by every means.

"It's still *drek*," Yankel retorted, "a quote full of it, Mr. Charis-Fourier-Bakunin. Now I will give you something very simple; a real quote that makes sense even for the stupid— Charis: 'To no one according to his needs, to no one according to his disability!' "

"And who said that, *groise petzl*?"

"And who do you think said that?" asked Yankel

"As if I don't know. It was not you, *groise petzl*!"

"So you know? So what? So who said it?"

"Your German economist, whom you also hate; that swindler, Karl Marx. He stole all of his basic theories from that Englishman, David Ricardo. A *klipe*—shrewing up us anarchists!"

"Some *lamdn* you are, you stupid scholar!" said Yankel. "I intentionally misquoted Marx."

"And that makes you even a more special *petzl*!"

Some of the quieter patrons of the café, reading their papers, began protesting. Vile language was not to be tolerated. Big pricks or little pricks—this was a reflective, intellectual café, a place in which to rest, to discuss, to argue quietly. A few patrons came over to Yankel and Charis. They admonished them, shaking fingers. They sneered at their shouting or shouted back at the two shouters. "Shut up!" "*Zay Shtil*, scholars!" said two, going back to their papers.

I left, to go to other cafés. I had sold a few papers and magazines. I had a head knocking against itself, wondering what sort of game Yankel and Charis were playing. It was a game of quotes, I decided. I thought of returning in a few days, going to the library at Seward Park, looking up Karl Marx and Fourier, copying down something important—and then, suddenly, I would become a quoter; a quiet quoter, not concerned with becoming a *groise petzl*. I would be a *lamdn*—a scholar.

A few days later, selling papers again at the scholarly Yankel-Charis Café, as I began to call it, I heard them at it again. This time, Charis, an equally insulting orator when he got started, was orating—pointing up Yankel's major physical deficiencies. They were everywhere.

"You should have lived in the time of Brook Farm, Mr. Karl Marx Yankel. You would, then, have been a taller man. Not herring—but natural food. Not meat, but dairy. You would have had great locks of hair instead of being a baldy; a mouth that had teeth, so you could bite on a piece of bread; a nose that was not always running. You could, Yankel, have been a polished anarchist—like me. Yes, like me!"

178

"Like you? A *maggid*—wanderer—preaching anarchism to cows and sheep, *nokh*. What else, Sir François Marie Charles Fourier—with your *dreky* communes? All right, buy me another glass of tea; another lox and bagel. Try and bribe me! Well, bribe me—what are you waiting for? And while you're bribing me, I'll go and *pish* a little bit," said Yankel, heading for the toilet.

When he returned there was the tea, not the lox and bagel. Yankel sighed, said that he was hungry and Charis ordered the rest.

When it came, Charis said quietly: "I'll tell you who visited and wrote about Brook Farm. When did I learn about it? Maybe yesterday? Maybe last year? What difference does that make? I remember what I like to recall. To Brook Farm there came—let me say it, *mamzer*—men like Horace Greeley. You don't like him? He published Karl Marx, Mr. Karl Marx Yankel. What are you—a Yankelist? All right, how about Charles A. Dana? How about Orestes Bronson? Oh, you don't like Catholics, Protestants, Muslims—and even some Jews? What do you like just lox and bagels?"

Yankel, eating the bagel, sipping the tea, filling himself up for an assault on his friend, Charis, suddenly belched. He was very good at belching and farting, especially when he had a mouth full of food. Now finished, he said: "Charis, you're not only an illiterate quoter, an obnoxious anarchist, a totally anti-social creature of the upper and lower darkness—but you pretend that you know about the elite. Such fancy names you give me! Who do you think Horace Greeley was? A cultured anti-Semite—that's all. Oh, you don't like that? Do you know what Karl Marx wrote—and I am not a Marxist, you dolt! You call me that—so call me that! I am my own revolutionist. Yes, a Yankelist. I take a little from here, a little from there, but I am Yankel, just plain Yankel. And if you call me Mr. Karl Marx Yankel again, I'll slap your dirty *ponem*—you filthy Brook Farmist! What is the point in quoting anything to you, Charis? You'll get it all wrong to begin with—and you'll never

179

remember it by tonight. Do you know what I would have gotten from Brook Farm—*gornisht mit leber*. Not even lox, Charis. Nothing with liver is all Brook Farm was worth; just another hopeless experiment in American utopianism. It would have been better had they created Brook Farm on East Broadway, near Seward Park, where we could sit and look at cows, see a piece of nature that is not made of stone, instead of all this manure and just horses shitting in the streets.''

Brook Farm still meant nothing to me, though horses dirtying up the streets meant a lot. I often had to walk through their leavings, which my sister called dung and Yankel called shit. It was a matter of bad taste.

I often felt that Yankel and Charis were really one body, one face, with two split minds. Maybe they were lunatics? If so, they represented quite a few people around the cafés that I sold my papers in. When I was not looking at either Yankel or Charis, when they spoke I could hardly tell them apart. They were a duet except in their differences regarding anarchism and Yankel's private revolutionary conceptions—whatever they were. Charis was certainly cleaner than Yankel—which was simple enough to be—and more concerned with nature than Yankel was. Yankel talked endlessly about wages, though he never earned a cent at anything. He was a *shnorrer* begging his way toward his secret revolutions; begging his way around the cafés; taking this, that, arguing for his tea, stealing a paper, disorderly, yet very knowing about all things as he zealously kibitzed his route through the Lower East Side cafés.

It was give, take, quote and misquote—then a frenzy of Yiddish and English to reach some vain and vague point. And yet it was not looked upon as comedy by either of them. If they laughed, which I seldom saw them do, it was some interior laughter not related to their arguments. It was public speaking; a platform of external raillery—to brand each other with their special nonsense. It enchanted me because they were part of that small group, the arguers—all egotists. They often stood in front of my mother's newsstand at the synagogue on the corner of

Madison and Montgomery—shouting and yelling. The anarchists
were always doing that, exploding as they read something in
their favorite journal. Nobody—anarchist, socialist or Yankelist
—was ten feet tall. They were half of that plus a few inches
more; and fat, from too much bread and potatoes; from sitting
forever; squat men waiting for New York to fall apart—at last.

These were my extra-extra revolutionists who belonged to
nothing organized or disorganized. But there were hundreds of
others, organized, Russian in spirit, hanging onto everything happening in the Russian *Gosudarstvennaya*—the imperial Duma;
that vague parliament organized after the Revolution of 1905.
It had been dissolved several times whenever the socialists in it
challenged the tsarist government. I heard strange names from
Charis and Yankel . . . and I thought no more about the Russians
with big names. It was another country. We had a country called
the Lower East Side, with our nonrevolutionary socialists leading
us to strikes and to the elections.

I did not meet the bomb-revolutionists. They had killed a few
past Presidents—and others; some capitalists and others. More
attempts had been made, but not by Charis or Yankel, who would
merely talk about it forever. When I did not meet them at the
cafés, I ran into them at the Chatham Square Library, where I
would take out novels about the early American frontier. There,
at the big tables, were dignified old men, with high starched collars, worn suits, and gold chains dangling from their vests. They
were writing furiously, having done some research for articles
and editorials for the various Yiddish newspapers three blocks
away. As far as I knew, they might also be revolutionists—if
cleaner ones; less animated, getting words down on sheets of
paper; bearded, gracious men, who were also baldheaded and
scratched away a bit at their bald heads between sentences,
phrases, and paragraphs. If they were agitated it was mostly by
the noise coming from Charis and Yankel arguing at another
table. Loud, in their normal custom, they were stopped occasionally by the librarian or *shushed* at by some irate Yiddish
journalists.

181

There had been a war recently in Europe between the Turks and the Russians. There had been little Balkan wars. The Japanese and the Russians had fought a war—earlier. Wars were everywhere—as conversation. I heard about it at home—*di milkhome*. The war, however, was not in the ghetto, as yet. It was in my books about Clive in India. It was on the frontier of an earlier America. It was romantic and hardly a bloody thing to me then. It was in half the speeches that Charis and Yankel made to each other—and what they would do when another war came.

Ah, what revolutionists! What diatribes and denunciations! What masks for other masks! And I heard Yankel say, when he wanted to set the record straight—for Charis's eccentric angles of anarchism—another quote: "On the whole it is safe to say that the early utopian theories and communistic colonies had but little influence on the formation of the modern socialist movement in the United States."

"Who wrote that *drek*?"

"Morris Hillquit, Sir François Marie Charles Fourier!"

"Hillquit is not worth the *tukhes* of Fourier! He is a businessman!"

"Fourier was the same with his communes!" barked Yankel. "All ass!"

And so I delivered my papers and wandered around the cafés after school with the late editions or the afternoon papers. I listened to small men and tall men, to the badly dressed and the neater, to scholars and madmen, to the doers and the talkers, to the eccentrics and the normal. It was hard to tell the difference, then. Now we have psychiatrists to tell us some of the differences between the normal and the abnormal. But Charis talked and Yankel talked; noisily, scholarly, in an endless turmoil of revolutionary blueprints, with nimble quotations created on the spot. Papers came out of jackets, overcoats, inner linings, and underwear. One baldheaded, short, and shaggy; the other neater, taller, anarchistic; a contrast in seriousness or comedy; two of the many hundreds that I saw in the cafés; two I got to know of the many more I was to know; talkers, doubters, strugglers—and before World War One began. Soon after that, by 1918, there would be revolutions starting all over Europe— and the Russians would make one with their Charises and Yankels sharing their theories, bombs, blood, and death.

Chapter 13

The Cafés—Tea, Strudel, and Monologues

A café, to my father, was a place where they served tea and talk, mixing unequal doses of philosophy, indignant politics, diatribes against some union leader, reverence for some rabbi, endless anger about sweatshop conditions—and whatever else was in the newspapers that evening. The cafés had various physical shapes, smells, characters, for all sorts of strange things went on there. A man could get himself married by proxy; or divorced, if not by proxy; or another job—everything that a harassed man needed or did not need. The mixture went with the coffee, the tea, the strudel—and ten languages, with English broken into bits and served along with the strudel.

The cafés were often stinking saloons, smelly damp cellars that made the beer, the kvass, and the schnapps taste sour. There were barrels containing wine—and men sat on them as if they had sprouted up, glass in hand, with an open mouth. On Cherry Street, Water Street, Front Street, were the worst cafés—worst, that is, for your eyes and nose. I rushed by to get out of the way of drunks. There were young children bringing home a pint of beer, trying not to spill too much—or have it taken away from them by an overly drunk drunk out of money. The filthier the café, the greater the air of mystery, but, too often, the more violent. My father would say: "So avoid them when you are selling papers. Anyway, what kind of Jew would find himself in one of those bedeviled places? He would have to be half a *goy* at least!"

Half a *goy*, whole a *goy*, whole a Jew—the cafés were the living centers of a liquid culture flowing from some earnest immigrant's soul. There, free, with friends, with tea or beer, depending on his moral involvements or his political and religious complexes, he spent some hours distilling regions of his mirth and misery. It was easy to be both mirthful and miserable within a minute in response to the sights inside or outside. Inside, many were drunk, if it was a café or a saloon for drinkers; outside, as if veering off by its own immediate folkways, were brawling men —local citizens of the street—Poles, Russians—but seldom the Irish. They had their own national conceits about where to drink and brawl and with whom they wanted to be. But once out of the saloons, they were in the gutters, often being dragged out of the way of a horse. The seasons, in the saloons did not matter; winter snow, ice, rain—it was the season of the belly full to the brain—and back again. The wages went and so did the drinker's liver and the food for his family. Everything went in a hurry. Mothers and children would be outside the saloons, coaxing a father to come home. The family brawls added to the simpler fights of drunks suddenly out of money, intensifying either their lassitude or their beery belligerence—and then came the cops.

There were also cafés for domino players who drank nothing alcoholic and seldom talked. The game was everything to them —until an argument suddenly changed the nontalkers into enemies. But the serious cafés were, usually, up one flight on Division Street, Allen Street, Orchard Street, Canal Street, or on very-broad Chatham Square. I was not to learn about the Café Royale until I was much older and a grown client among the

186

actors, actresses, playwrights, *shnorrers*, fund-raisers, chorus women, poets—and all the rest of the ego-centered intelligentsia and businessmen.

In the cafés it was a mishmash scene of large-sized newspapers and small-sized faces behind them. The newspapers created another world one flight up, especially in their tragic stories about the cities, towns, and villages the readers came from—in Eastern Europe. With the paper came a glass of tea, if the reader was in a hurry and wanted some brief escape. The accents on a man's real intensity occurred when he poured the tea into the saucer, slurped it, then gestured—if the news was bad—depending on his slurping powers. The tea consumption took place in one beautiful motion, Yiddish in style. The reader–tea-drinker had a special image, drafted from many interior sources. Up ahead, a chair away, was another large newspaper. Behind it, another man, more tea—and sounds of wrath or joy coming from him. Newspapers, glasses of tea, and echoes of rage made up the variegated monologues of the café's character.

Cafés and saloons opened early and closed late. Many sold food—bean soup, borsht, cold fish, Russian dishes, Jewish dishes, and something pronounced as *samitsh*. Tea came out of samovars in classical Russian style. The sugar was in an open bowl—huge lumps, unbroken, hardly the squares of today. Granulated sugar was impossible, unthinkable, with Jewish drinkers of tea. The lemon, too, was sucked when it was not put into the glass. The newspapers, the tea, the food, and the talk that never ended made some geniuses—and they were not the hand-clappers.

The talkers were men of extraordinary abilities—as talkers. Talk was the major art of the cafés with these aristocrats of rhetoric, the bringers of useless data, as they competed with their compote-quotes about all things of value. In this free arena, this circus without measure, it was the clacque that each man had that denoted the worth of the speaker-orator-lecturer-statesman-*shnorrer*. It was private meandering, public pontificating—and no decisions; for the talk went on for weeks or until one speaker suddenly decided that the dead end was truly dead.

187

Running out of his audience, he moved to another café. There he built another circus with newer spectators, philosophers—and kibitzers, for they could not always be told apart easily.

Socialists hung around with socialists—not Republicans. But socialists and anarchists, besides having their own cafés, had cafés in common for talking over their insurmountable divisions of heart, mind and politics. Within their midst were the Bundists and Zionists—with the Bundist, a Jewish socialist, wanting a Yiddish culture no matter where the Jews happened to live, and the Zionists, including the Labor Zionists, wanting Zion—and no other nation for their permanent spiritual home.

It has often been said that, in a café, two arguing Jews, when differing, could form three political parties . . . and I listened to all in the cafés, as the speakers and listeners interjected, projected, saluting an idea momentarily—only to give it up a week later when they were, for just another week, "converted" again. Yet every change of mind had within it the basis of the previous week's social and political ideals. What had changed was some symbol or some symbolical figure, or a new reference that no longer brought forth reverence for a man. A new social hero was created over a tenth glass of hot tea drunk from a cooling saucer.

It was hard, without my father's intrusion, for me to know one symbol from another. I learned to know the half black from the dark white but not the subtle distinctions between various forms of Zionism and socialism. In the overheated or overly cold cafés, where everybody sat with his hat and coat on, I would see men drop a penny into a box collecting money for this organization or that organization in Palestine. The collection offices were usually on East Broadway—where every stoop floor housed one of the dozens of collecting agencies—and the cafés were the main source for their future penny-revenues. Some boxes, said my father, just supported the collectors on East Broadway. Other boxes supported old rabbis, rabbinical schools, and yeshivas.

The collectors going to and from the cafés did not need to identify themselves or the essence of their charity, for the proprietor knew them as religious *shnorrers*, and he would nod. The collector took the old box, put a new one in its place—and out he went, heading for another sympathetic café. He had a notebook listing them, and a large black case into which went the *pushke*, as my mother called the little tin box. No key, no lock —just an opening on top for anything up to a quarter, and a place in the back where the *pushke* could be opened with the thumb and the index finger.

I heard about Theodore Herzl in the cafés. Some cafés had photos of Herzl, the author of a little pamphlet, ''The Jewish State.'' In his despairing letters, as Herzl wandered between kings, emperors, sultans, statesmen—the world of men who made decisions—he wrote one day in anger to a friend: ''I do not need rich Jews—what I need is men. *Donnerwetter*, they are hard to find. . . . Every day I observe with painful attention the sufferings of our people in every land. I believe that this pressure is bound to make men out of even the most abject wretches. . . .''

The men, and the ''wretches'' that I saw in the cafés, were, some thirty-four years later, to create Israel—the state Herzl dreamed of and spent his life struggling to bring to birth . . . and I heard about it in the making at the cafés. But in the cafés everybody was a dreamer, including many of the semi-ragged workers sipping tea, worrying about forty separate fantasies connected with the next day's work; the despair of their homes, sick children, and the tenement within the icebox of their souls. An hour at a café, with a friend, and spiritual talk, made the next day livable, if not quite human.

I heard the word *aliyah* and I confused it with the word, *aliye*, which meant going up to the pulpit to take part when the Scroll of the Torah was read. Later, I was to learn that *aliyah* was related to *The Lovers of Zion*, those who migrated in the latter part of the nineteenth century to Palestine, to dig the soil and prepare Palestine for what in 1948 was to become Israel, and that many of my relatives, from Russia and Poland, had gone in the Second and the Third *Aliyah*—the later migrations to Palestine. But it was more than a word to the talkers in the cafés.

189

HARRY ROSKOLENKO

It was a violent point of denunciation, depending on whether one was a Bundist and another was a Zionist. Some of the talkers had even gone to Switzerland, to a Zionist Congress, and they talked, talked, talked—and I sold, sold, and sold my newspapers. I listened, getting bits of this, less of that—then asked questions when I got home, about *that*.

The cafés were forums, soapboxes, lecture halls, auditoriums, for the argumentative Jews—and there were many of these. Ideas about God, the synagogue, the union, intermeshed. It was difficult, then, for me to see how some men could be two things— like Zionist-anarchists; or Zionists who were also atheists; or socialists who were Zionists and atheists. It was like a chess game—with no rules. But since the cafés were a world away from work and home, the intermeshing malcontents, not satisfied with being just one thing, made all of my confusions quite normal. Who was not at least two or three separate spiritual and physical entities on the Lower East Side? My father managed socialism, orthodoxy, and Zionism, quite easily, and so did the kibitzers and the serious, who could stay up late if the next day was a holiday. They were as normal as the next man—and the next man was in every café where I sold my papers.

It was mostly a man's subjective world in the cafés. Some women came, and their less violent and tidier presence within these café-castles, made up of old chairs and cigarettes, calmed a café briefly. The odors changed. Perfume was used by the most radical women, and their minutes of femininity made a moment of romantic talk possible. But the men, mostly married, had other urges—most of them not libidinous. They were married to politics. The visting women, if virginal, remained that way, giving their bodies to causes. I never heard of a scandal, nor did my father mention any in his typical briefing of my mind, my walks, my habits—and my newspaper routes. But I might not have been listening too well or my thoughts were about the East River, the boats and ships and steam—and that one day I would stow away and see more than the Lower East Side and its cafés. These cafés had no sea captains, no mates, no Jack Londons—

190

only pale men, heavily mustached and bearded, their eyes shining, their talk ego-sodden, their voices breaking over their cigarettes into tubercular rasping, and their idealism coughing up God, Man, and the Devil—as political partners.

The men wore large black hats, bowlers, starched collars, even when they were poor and dirty. The combination was like a uniform without which they might have been naked. They talked *talk*, listened to half of an answer, especially if the answer was something they did not like at the moment; or they listened to themselves, not all amazed that they were so eloquent, witty, and learned. Without doubt, everybody was a scholar.

The cafés were named after their European cities, villages, streets, and towns. There was, I recall, the Odessa Café on East Broadway, a few thousand miles from its original geography. Others were called Krakow, Moscow, Kiev, Lublin, and Warsaw. As for the saloons on Cherry Street, they were nameless—just drunken customers and a number painted over a dirty window. In the cafés, not in the saloons, a client chess player, reader, or talker could receive his mail—especially if he was a boarder or he left his wife. He could also be served with a summons there, and I once heard my mother say to my father, "Tante Blima is going to get a *get*"—a divorce. Yosel, her husband, had been served at the Odessa Café on East Broadway, while eating borsht.

What a world of no secrets! A man just walked in, sat down, and started his permanent argument. If no one was about he would practice on himself before another sitter arrived to engage him in fantasy, poetry, politics, and other forms of spiritual searching. Their fur coats, old, and fur hats, older, made a pile on a chair. Nails on the walls were the hangers, but chairs were better—and then came the pogroms, the belches, the seltzer water, as interludes between other disasters. Around the talkers were bits of lemon, crumbs of cake, wetted lumps of sugar—and ten more eloquent disasters in the talking, en route.

I never knew the card players or the gamblers, for that kind of café was not within my walking-talking-visiting route. I saw the pockets of ragged poets and heard their poems read to each

191

other. I saw the storytellers scribbling phrases and paragraphs, then putting the pencils to their lips to wet them down for more scribbling. Some merely talked their stories and invented as they went, to write them later; but if the reaction was good enough they would discuss the merits of a phrase and some characterization. They were the literary ones, often very silent, scrawling away, looking up at a fly, watching the fly fly—then going back to pieces of worn-out paper or shabby notebooks to delineate more. And, too often, when I went out selling papers and approached one of the scribblers, he would look up angrily, then say, "Why aren't you in *cheder*? Is your father so poor that you must spend your studying time selling papers?" I would say *no, yes, perhaps*—to make him buy a paper. It was hardly a lie—just Jewish ambivalence. The next questions were—"Who is your father? Where does he come from? What is his synagogue? All right, give me *The Stick*."

More often a scribbler would borrow a paper, turn it around and about, look it over, then give it back—without saying thanks. If they said thanks they were odd people. They had merely looked and that cost nothing . . . but, as happened once, a scribbler said to me, "Listen—that is my poem in the paper." He read what was printed in a little squared-off box. Loud, proud, glancing about. Then I said, "Buy the paper—buy!" The second "buy" sold him the paper.

There were bohemian cafés where wine took the place of politics and free love replaced religious demands. I saw those who frequented them, deep in the cellars, pre-Greenwich Village, without too many taboos, noisy with dancers and accordionists. I never went in—for there were no Yiddish readers there. I merely looked in, edging down the sagging wooden stairs, breathing anxiously, seeing what must have been an East Side conception of Paris on Division Street, with women, their skirts raised, and their thighs showing amid flaring petticoats. Outside, as if it were part of the social arrangements, were the prostitutes. My father called them *kurvas*—and I was not to go near them, which made them all the more mysterious. I did not know what they did; but they stood on corners, walked down and up, talked to men coming up from the cellars, walked away with them, hugging an old friend, laughing, then disappearing into a shabby building—and that was all I knew or saw.

By the time I went to sea, at thirteen, and I saw the same sort of cafés in London and Hamburg, my father's warnings were modestly known to me. But then, on Division Street, the prostitutes were just beautiful women walking with men. My father's phrases were just my father's phrases—and he had them for everything I did or did not do. Some were semidemands—to be the good son. Others were even more so—decisions. Don't go near the Irish—for my papers would be torn and my nose would be flattened out.

These were the cafés of my childhood—ghostly places, remembered smells, bearded faces old and studious; and these were the places that attuned my senses; a boy and his eyes looking at things that were either sickening or magical. The world was all there, rushing about in scattering images—voices, faces, bodies —then talk, talk, talk . . . and it was not until the late 1920s, when I was twenty years of age, that I was to go to the Café Royale—Second Avenue's Algonquin, for the headier discussions of another time. By this time I was the Marxist who had seen and lived in many seaports of the world; a third mate when I quit the sea so that I could study, write poetry, talk about Trotsky, Stalin, Lenin, Rosa Luxemburg, Karl Marx—the elite of revolutions planned, made, lost—and I was to remember Charis, the anarchist of the cafés, whom I knew when I was seven and eight—and Yankel, his collaborator in noisy theories —the *shnorrers* of 1914, just before the war ended my romantic view of the world across the Atlantic Ocean.

At the Café Royale one saw every actor, playwright, poet, and revolutionary; every name from Second Avenue's massive Yiddish drama of a street. Every sitter talked with a majestic pause, acting around some pickled herring, black bread, and tea. But the Royale would close up one day after another war. The poets and the others would be gone—and another era dead. The café

193

and the era, when done, would sweep away people and a language that had been in all the senses. The café died like the sitters—dead within itself. After the café's closing one of the oldest sitters would attempt suicide—for he had no other home. A second would die in his apartment amid ten thousand books on Americana—the specialty of a man whose real language was Russian-Yiddish. The café itself would become a cleaning store, an American-enough symbol of sanitation, if without the glass of tea and the lemon.

There were still other cafés, and these were considered odd to the proletariat and the immigrants—like Little Hungary, founded by Max Schwartz at 259 East Houston Street, near Liberty Hall. Actually Little Hungary was odd because it was here that the political conservatives came to talk Republican Party politics at the turn of the century and to challenge everything after 1901. It had the atmosphere of Budapest, the feel of the Danube, in its music, with Liszt going with the paid-for goulash and the free-lunch sandwiches. A radical-conservative visitor, Theodore Roosevelt, came there for dinner one night— for the Jewish vote. When Prohibition strangled New York's drinkers, the Little Hungary gave a party, opened its cellars, emptied them into the guests for free—and closed up forever.

Cafés on art, politics, and bread—and every social philosophy; shabby places, too often; nations within a city in little and large rooms. Cellars, parlor floors, street floors—and open doors for everyone. The cafés gave the Lower East Side a head, a body, a mind—and a brilliance that is brutally missing today. It created a language and it killed a language. It inherited the migrations and the men who created industries along with their basic arts. The image of another time completes itself. The *then* is *gestorbn* —dead.

Chapter 14
Politicians and Propagandists

The nimblest politicians around our streets were the walking-takers. As professional pedestrians looking for something to take—or sell—the street was their natural habitat. Besides selling us their big political parties around Election Day, their conceits about democracy included taking anything handy.

The cops, with their long mustaches and their Bobby helmets, had it easiest. They took fruit from the vendors, newspapers, chewing gum, beer, shirts, ties—anything that was in a store or on a pushcart. It was natural, normal—and it helped their methods of policing. It was a bribe, and everybody bribed, not to be bothered. The milkman, rattling his bottles, who collected once a week, came away with home-made cakes or a Yiddish lecture. The iceman took whatever he could get after walking up five flights of stairs with his dripping wooden bucket. If he had time, he got a glass of hot tea from an overbusy *baleboosteh*, who could do everything better than nurses, doctors, dentists, the politicians, and the iceman.

The politicians came in various natural disguises. There were the Irishmen outside the corner saloons—and every corner, or all four, had saloons—for that was the only cultural and physical reason for having a corner. And every corner was a political island alive with beer, whiskey, drunks—and the inherent rhetoric of a social club without walls, where men moved about the open streets like so many birds whirling over the manure heaps in the gutters.

Of course, there were the real politicians from Tammany Hall, not too far away. I thought, because they used Indian names, that they were reformed or renegade Indians, not Irishmen. But there were Jews and Germans, too, in Tammany Hall. What was a Jew doing among the Irish-Indians? He was a politician, which to us meant a crook. But I never saw a Jewish cop. The Jews were peddlers and the Irish were the cops who took from the peddlers—and all was not right on Cherry Street.

It seemed incomprehensible that a politician could also be a socialist. What had socialism to do with those one-flight-up political, unsavory clubs that inundated our streets? They were Tammany clubs—but hardly the club inspired by an Indian chief, who, centuries before, had welcomed an Englishman named William Penn. It was closer to P. T. Barnum, who had an Indian museum right in City Hall; or Aaron Burr, who had used Tammany when he ran for the Vice-Presidency. It was the Tammany of Fernando Wood, the mayor of New York in 1850, who had prepared Tammany for what it later became under Boss Tweed —the spawning ground for every sort of public and private corruption. And it had gone on like that under leaders like John Kelly, Richard Croker, Charles Murphy—all working from East Fourteenth Street, where Tammany Hall had its majestic lootery. In my boyhood, when I walked to East Fourteenth Street, I would find myself among the whores and the pimps, all getting favors, jobs, and protection at the stony wigwam across from the music halls.

In my home the word Tammany meant something crude, evil, and bad—a seven-letter word that had a much worse connotation than a four-letter word, which none of us ever used. But there were Jewish politicians in Tammany—so to hell, or to Gehenna, with them. There was John Purroy Mitchell, a Democrat and reformer opposed to Tammany Hall, of which he was not a member. And there was Alfred E. Smith who was between men like Mitchell. Smith was trying to make Tammany more moral, decent, clean—like a charitable organization doing good deeds among the poor. For Tammany Hall had so many forms of evil and magic that it was difficult to take something and then denounce the giver. It was a symbol of greed, nevertheless, despite the public displays its members put on as mustached saints of charity. One hand gave and ten hands took . . . and my father would spit, my mother would shake her head, and my sister Edna would offer up a small lecture—and that was Tammany Hall to all of us.

As for the socialists, we knew their immediate working-class relationships. As for the liberals, I did not hear about them until I was ten, when I passed the Liberal Club on Macdougal Street and wondered what they did inside their handsome building. But I knew the streets of the real politicians—every five blocks, up one flight, front and back, with Jewish ward-heelers, businessmen, consters—our kind, exerting their special bids for power, charity—and a fire and a flame to all of them, we said. We had a series of political myths, and so we damned them with joy. They were Judas goats, traitors, shifty. Their hands were made of glue. Their eyes were twisted in four directions. Their pockets were filled with thousand-dollar bills—and they said the various things to us like . . . "Is there something you need or that I can get for you?"

Since I could not vote at seven, it was as useless telling the politician that I wanted a catcher's glove, a pair of track shoes, or two weeks in the country. In fourteen more years I would be eligible for favors. But my father was asked by a Jewish member of Tammany Hall, "Is there a greenhorn that you want to bring over from Russia? Does he have a *shifskart*? How much does he need—twenty dollars? Here is ten—and remember Election Day. Vote! No, not socialist—Democratic Party!"

The appeal was made in Yiddish, English, German, Polish, Russian—and Democrat. The greenhorn, or a *griner tukhes*,

197

HARRY ROSKOLENKO

was a country cousin out of the country—in some *shtetl* in Russia or Poland. When he arrived, everything about him was green; his complexion, from the trip in steerage; his lack of knowledge, about where he was or where he was going. He was green down to his shoes and up to his hat—and for weeks my family became the great Americanizers-in-a-hurry. How to use the horsecars, subways, and the free baths. Where were the best bargains? On Orchard Street. Where were the worst hooligans? Anywhere west of Cherry Street. How did a *griner tukhes* get to City Hall? By magic. And when he talked to a cop, to please tip his hat in advance. What *verein* did one join or sick-and-death-benefit society? The one that gave you the most for the least, was my father's stock answer—his *verein*. Where did one find a flat? In a building that had a sign— "FLAT TO LET." A job? Well, that was very simple, said my father. "Follow me to my shop tomorrow morning. Now, have some schnapps—and go to sleep."

The greenhorn was asleep and tomorrow was another world. It would, soon enough, involve him in religion and socialism. Socialism seemed most natural, most related to the Old Testament, most given over to a man about to start sweating in a sweatshop. And the socialist most talked about was the socialist Meyer London, who lived on East Broadway, near the Arnold Toynbee House—a house created by the English anti-Marxist sociologist, who wanted to educate the workingman in improving his soul as well as his wages. Whether the adjacent house influenced Meyer London, we did not know. In later years, the Arnold Toynbee House was to become a *mikva*, a ritualarium for purifying women after menstruating. But between *mikvas*, soul-sodden houses, sociology, English charity, and Meyer London, the greenhorn was soon being advised by my father to vote for Meyer London in five years, when the greenhorn became a citizen.

There were nonsocialist politicians, Democrats like Samuel Dickstein and Dr. William Sirovich, an intellectual medicine man, who were running for various offices in the city, state, or in Washington. They looked awesome, forbidding, bourgeois, too

198

rich to me—not that our socialist politicians looked too poor. Meyer London looked like a lawyer turned into a moral intellectual. He spoke with fiery force—and we loved his socialist language. Meyer London was Samson, George Washington, Zane Grey—and the cop on the horse, to me.

The greenhorn cousins voted for Meyer London in 1914, when London, the first socialist to be elected to the House of Congress, became the permanent socialist symbol for the Lower East Side. Other men had run on the Socialist Party ticket before, especially Morris Hillquit, who had been beaten by Daniel De Leon's entrance as a candidate, De Leon's candidacy splitting the radical vote on the Lower East Side. But Election Day was one thing and being a member of the Socialist Party was another.

I heard about politics without politics—anarchism, with Bakunin whispered over as if he were Moses, Jesus, and God, and that no one should have a thing to do with the *state*.

State? Did they mean the United States? Was it New York State? No one explained it, nor did I know the right question to get the right answer. But there was Emma Goldman, fresh from Russia and Rochester, hardly a city to spawn anarchism. She advocated birth control, pacifism, free love—hardly Judaic. Her magazine, *Mother Earth*, found its way into our house along with *The Masses*—all Uncle Solomon's literature on the nature of man in and out of socialism and anarchism. When Emma Goldman spoke, and I was to hear her talk about pogroms in Russia, she filled the hall on Clinton Street—a flame of a woman bearing fire from Mount Emma Goldman. It was table talk, café talk, street and synagogue language—bringing the tsar, Russian Bolshevism, still in its pre-World War One stage, right into our glasses of tea.

But the politicians who got the petty things done for the Lower East Side were not the socialists, who could not, because they did not have the voting power of the Democrats and the Republicans. We got free milk from the Republicans and Democrats; others got free beer—from Tammany. Alfred E. Smith from Oliver Street, the Democratic leader in the State Assembly

199

HARRY ROSKOLENKO

when I was a child, was a much-loved politician, able to convince any number of East Side Jews that he was for them as much
as the socialists were. While hardly for socialism in any form,
he was against child labor and for various reforms that helped
to change the human picture in the sweatshops where my father
worked. When I went out with my newspapers, I would often
pass Smith's home on Oliver Street. I saw him once emerging
with his brown derby, his cigar, enter a car, wave to everybody
—and off he went to Tammany Hall's den of tigers, the permanent Irish circus on East Fourteenth Street.

The Socialists, powerless, ran nothing but some of the unions.
The Democrats had a variety of specialists, from actual sewers
through political sewers, and they made money on every contract let out by the City of New York, to build public buildings,
put up street lights, remove snow, make rain, put out fires, remove garbage, use garbage—and they came up from their sewers
to the tenements, which their men allegedly inspected. They were
paid off by the owners, and the fire hazards remained in the
five-, six-, and seven-story tenements with the wooden stairs, and
the wooden people—who would one day burn up. The Democrats ran the city, the fire department—and the fires, in the
winters, when entire blocks went up, were very democratic. Every
day had a fire, and they seemed to be a way of getting warm.
To the Socialists, who took out their wrath on the Democrats,
every fire was a moral issue. It was Old Testament anger boiling
up into volcanic politics—with justice and humanity ever to the
fore.

The dialogue about corruption was endless. One man was
honest, another dishonest. It went on over tea and coffee. It
was cake and *tsimmes* to us. When? Who? What? But it never
involved the socialists, said my father. They were good people
—and he would say it with some finality:

"Our Jewish socialists do not corrupt people," my father
stated over the tea—and he had never heard of Lord Acton.

"Who *corrupts* people?" I asked again. Even the word
sounded sickening, and I envisioned babies being tortured.

200

"People who do not believe in God, to begin with. People with too much money and no soul. People who want everything and give nothing back—they corrupt."

It was simple, ethical, religious, honorable—large enough to fit my little world into it. I believed, because my father said it . . . and I was against corruption, on and off, for the next fifty-five years. But politics and corruption were uncles, cousins, aunts —and bastards—all living on the same street, city and country . . . and the politicians of the Socialist Party, men like Meyer London and Morris Hillquit, stood for what my father wanted.

Morris Hillquit, the theoretician, was the first truly cultured socialist to run for a seat in Congress, we said with Jewish pride. Hillquit spoke many languages, my father said . . . and he had talked with him in Russian, German, and Yiddish. The socialists had a country full of men of honor. There was the incorruptible Eugene V. Debs, who took a drink or two and packed in the Jewish masses whenever he spoke in New York City during the big strikes. Debs had run for the presidency many times. In 1900 he got 96,000 votes. In 1904, 400,000 votes. In 1912, when Uncle Solomon voted, Debs received almost 900,000 votes. By then, the Socialist Party, a properly disloyal opposition, had many candidates running—to establish their mixture of radicalism, liberalism, and populism as the new century's emblems of social and political progress.

But it was Meyer London who took over my small sense of fantasy and reality. Perhaps it was the firm lines of his face? His glasses, pinched on his nose? His eloquence and gestures? In my fantasies, I related Meyer London to Jack London, equally heroic to me as a novelist. I had read *The Sea Wolf, White Fang, Burning Daylight, Martin Eden, The Iron Heel*—books brought home by my librarian sister, Edna, who superintended my hurried reading. Little did I then know the juxtapositions: London wrote about the sea, the sea was outside my window— and between these books and my street wanderings I was, in a few years, to feel all the inspirations attending both climates of adventure and idealism.

201

HARRY ROSKOLENKO

Both Londons were rebels, and my immediate geography created rebellion. My father was religious—and I found it constricting soon enough. As for Meyer London, our spokesman from East Broadway, he had been born in 1871, in the town of Kalvarja, not too far from the Prussian border. His father had been a rabbi, but he did not follow his father into the rabbinate. Instead, he followed his family to Suffolk Street and became an anarchist, then the editor of *Morning Star*. He had done many things en route to becoming our leader. As a lawyer, he fought for us, speaking in beautiful English, and that mattered and flattered us. As a student he had tutored others so that they could become like him, thereby touching our lives in every direction. He worked with the unions, especially my father's ILGWU—and brought my father's problems back into the kitchen and the living room. As a candidate for the State Assembly, against Tammany Hall, he ran from a district that included whorehouses, opium parlors, saloons by the dozens, ugly factories, terrifying tenements—and Tammany Hall itself, right in the district. His opposition was Tammany's massive collection of ward heelers, drunks, the lost poor, the two-dollar voters, criminals, pimps, their women—and the rest of the honest proletariat, middle-class and *lumpen* proletarians. London had enough crafts and professions to run against to make him the permanent hero of the Jewish masses—and socialism.

Morris Hillquit, astute theoretician, who much earlier had carried on discussions on the rooftops of Cherry Street tenements, was close enough by that tenement-token for us to accept his scholarly, nonrhetorical speeches. In one of his books, *Loose Leaves from a Busy Life*, he recalls the following:

"Peals of gay laughter and voices in earnest and animated conversations would come from different groups on the roofs, while the melancholy and nostalgic strains of popular Russian folk songs would often resound in the still evening air. It was a slice of old Russian life that was transported to Cherry Street. . . ."

Arriving in New York during the 1880s, Morris Hillquit, cul-

202

tured, gentle, logical, hard-working, debated, wrote, and lectured about socialism. He was a withdrawn man, after a fashion; the interior intellectual, very difficult to reach, my father would say; hardly the passionate man that London was; more the logician of socialist thoughts, values, and theories. When we went to hear him at the Educational Alliance or across from the *Daily Forward*, in Seward Park, we heard a gentle person tell us what our lives were like; and he would, with the same continuous logic, tell us what socialism would do for us.

Born in Riga, familiar with many languages, a consumptive, reviled on occasion by his own party, considered a municipal socialist concerned with the subways and the sewage systems under our streets—he was hardly the radical of the party, but he had his own gentler following in our midst. A parliamentarian of many gifts, he was, with men like my Uncle Solomon backing him, to steer the Socialist Party into its major split. One wing after World War One went Bolshevik-Communist; the other remained strictly parliamentarian. And what Hillquit had learned from the rooftops, where Uncle Solomon sang along with him, was to keep Branch 17 of the Socialist Party—strictly a Russian-speaking branch—out of the reach of the Communists when the split took place after the Russian Revolution.

Emma Goldman, hardly a friend of Morris Hillquit, had this to say in her book, *Living My Life*: "When I first came to New York, I used to attend joint gatherings of anarchists and socialists, among whom there were also the two brothers Hilkowitch. One occasion of those days had been particularly memorable. It was a Yom Kippur celebration, held as a protest against Jewish orthodoxy. Speeches on free thought, dances, and plenty of eats took the place of the traditional fast and prayers. Religious Jews resented our desecration of their holiest Day of Atonement, and their sons came down in strong force to meet our boys in pitched battle. . . . While the affray was going on in the street, anarchist and socialist orators were holding forth inside the hall, young Morris Hilkowitch having the floor at that time. . . ."

What Emma Goldman had to say hardly taxed Morris Hillquit intellectually. What the Democrats and Republicans had to say was not better. He had a logic they did not have. Though hardly emotionally eloquent, his intellectual force made him the Socialist Party candidate for mayor twice, but he never held an elective office . . . and my father would say, half in criticism and half in admiration, "Hillquit *patshket*. He plays around beautifully with the languages, but where is he getting us? We need men who do not always talk theories. Meyer London is better for us."

Hillquit, sophisticated, flexible, had in 1890 begun a paper called the *Arbeiter Zeitung*. Eight hundred dollars had been his working capital. One of his editors was Abraham Cahan, soon to be the editor, the shaker, the innovator, and the inventor of the greatest Yiddish newspaper, *The Forward*. Hillquit debated all sorts of people about socialism, including a Catholic professor, John A. Ryan, who taught economics and moral theology. At the Economics Club of New York he debated Professor Edwin R. A. Seligman of Columbia University . . . and Seligman, when following Hillquit to the speaker's platform, said, as he noticed Hillquit's expensive watch: "Ladies and gentlemen, this golden watch belongs to the representative of the proletariat, while I, a representative of the bourgeoisie, wear an Ingersoll dollar watch."

Hillquit, when his time came for rebuttal, answered: "See how the bourgeoisie takes everything away from the proletariat! Professor Seligman has taken away my golden watch and left me his Ingersoll. . . ." It was like that with Morris Hillquit, but logic was not enough, even socialist logic. He hardly looked like a bona fide resident of the Lower East Side or a socialist. He was too fastidious, too much the scholar, too aloof—and I would stare at him at the Educational Alliance and wonder why he was one of us and not in the parties of Teddy Roosevelt, Woodrow Wilson, Alfred E. Smith—or Hylan—all very good bourgeois indeed.

Every union had its odd score of self-servers and politicians— and they went together. Some were poets and playwrights. There were men like Morris Winchefsky, writer, speaker, and unionist, who was called the "grandfather" of Jewish socialism. Winchefsky was to go from anarchism to socialism and Communism before he died—a route many an adventuring politician for the proletariat was to take later on. The man everybody knew was Abraham Cahan, especially for his politics and his journalistic feats. Scathing, moralistic, anti-Bolshevik and anti-Communist, a sort of socialist William Randolph Hearst, as well as a novelist of high stature, Cahan knew his Lower East Side—and what to offer his ambivalent readers. His imposing novel, *The Rise of David Levinsky*, gave him an audience that included more than the Jews in New York.

He had his detractors and those who loved him, for his journalistic ironies and Yiddish warmth. When he arrived in New York during the 1880s, there were about 250,000 Jews in the city, but without a Yiddish newspaper or a journal of ideas and socialist thought. Cahan eventually was to supply both, and my mother was to point him out when we went to *The Forward* with our little red cart to haul a few hundred copies to our newsstand. He was Abe Cahan, the innovator, not too theoretical, totally Yiddish in his thoughts, values, expressions—and his newspaper expressed facets of his many admixtures in style and personality. He had his own language, grafted out of bread, herring, and steel. He was imposing in a short sort of way, with the look of an editor endlessly looking for something different and exciting. Had the Old Testament not yet been written, Cahan would have arranged for it with a writer or would have done it himself. The love-hate medium encased within his authoritarian manner of writing the drama reviews and the editorials shook up more than East Broadway and Second Avenue.

I would see him, and then off we would march with the little red cart. "So that is Abraham Cahan. He looks like Uncle Solomon—but smaller. . . ." My mother answered, "He's bigger!" The bigness of Cahan included, by association, the men he had met and argued with—men like Anatole France and Alfred Dreyfus; for Cahan was a cosmopolitan among cosmopolitans on East Broadway. In his youth, when he was a revolutionary under

205

the tsar—he once said, as he touched a brochure that had been printed in the underground by Russian revolutionaries, "A forbidden object, its publishers are those . . . who live together like brothers and are ready to go to the gallows for freedom and justice. This knowledge had an indescribable influence on me, and the danger connected with reading this brochure enhanced its magnetism. I touched the little book as one touches a holy thing. . . ."

He had met with Lenin in Krakow in 1912—and they talked American politics. He knew the leaders of the world and the writers, and he published many of them in his paper—Max Nordau, Zionist; August Bebel, a German socialist leader; Karl Liebknecht, who led a German Communist revolution and was murdered; Arnold Bennett, the English novelist. The names of the people Cahan knew became like a filing cabinet; and my father would say to my mother, "He is a great man. Sell more of his papers." What a fatherly demand!

Every Jewish and Yiddish writer of merit and genius was eventually to appear in Cahan's paper, including many Gentiles. There was Karl Kautsky and Jean Longuet. There were the Singers—Bashevis, and his brother, I. J. Singer, who was to write *Yoshe Kalb* for *The Forward*—for it was our *Atlantic Monthly*, *American Mercury*, and *Hound & Horn*—written in classical and colloquial Yiddish and much more radical. Up at the top of the Forward Building, he steered a paper he had created through half of an American century—for immigrants.

But he was a politician by nature; an explosive one; the journalist, the editor, and the socialist delegate to international conventions. There he would battle socialist anti-Semitism and write dialectically against rising Communism; and though he had once been a revolutionary, he was to turn from the Communists with anger. In 1881, when Tsar Alexander II was assassinated, Cahan, then with the revolutionaries, expected a revolt. When he left Russia and came to New York's ghettos, he soon found himself deep in the middle of debates and socialist organizations, talking Russian, German, and Yiddish; and he

206

was to say one day in 1884: "It is a joke. I debate, I argue, I get excited, I shriek, and in the middle of all this I remind myself that I am a vacant vessel, an empty man without a shred of knowledge, and I begin to blush. I am ashamed of myself."

Once when Cahan was addressing a meeting of strikers in Philadelphia, a colleague, Leon Kobrin, the playwright and novelist, recorded the following: "Cahan, dressed in a Prince Albert with clean white cuffs, lashed out at the strikebreakers: 'Such girls should be laid down and flogged; their flesh should be torn from them piece by piece . . . to remember forever not to scab for your bloodsuckers!' The girls trembled and the crowd roared with pleasure." And Cahan, finishing, yelled out, "Hooray for socialism." It was like a football game, left-wing style. Finally, "paraphrasing the Hebrew prayer, he said, 'And Zion shall be redeemed.' "

This was in part the man, the socialist, the editor, the politician, who would never hold public office. He did not have to—not from his savagely sentimental seat in the Forward Building at 175 East Broadway. I was to sell his paper, listen to him roar, listen to him purr, see him among the *shnorrers*, poets, agitators, peddlers, pressers—the proletariat—us, down there, below East Broadway.

But there were so many politicians and poets and propagandists—all tied together by socialism and Zionism. There was Joseph Barondess, born of a Hasidic family, who helped build the cloakmakers' union, about whom Leon Kobrin would say one day: "Not one of that period had so many Hasidim among the workers as Barondess." Barondess, instead of attacking the capitalists, abused the workers into action. Kobrin recollects: "In the cursed Russia under the Tsar, you traded with the Gentiles on the market and earned a few pennies a week. Only on Saturday could you afford a little meat. So you think that your miserable pay in a sweatshop, given to you by the cockroach bosses, is a lot. But I want to tell you that in America this is hunger wages. You could earn ten times as much if you were not such jackasses. . . . You are in America, and not in *Shnipi-*

207

shok, Tuneadefke, or *Blutofke"*—imagined names that Barondess remembered had been created by Mendele Mokher Seforim, the earliest and greatest Yiddish folklorist. "Here you can live like human beings! Eat like human beings! Be dressed like human beings! . . . were you not such cows, such oxen, such jackasses! . . ."

Who was not a politician or a propagandist? We had a ghetto full, masked and unmasked, to enlist the energies of socialists, Democrats, Republicans—and zany people. They were socialist lawyers and labor leaders; secretaries and treasurers in The Workmen's Circle and benefit societies. They were all in politics up to their bald heads, convincing Jewish workers they would never become bosses, small or large; that they were workers, not members of the growing middle class—and the names of some of these poets, playwrights, novelists, labor leaders, demagogues, exact and inexact socialists, were, among the hundreds, men like B. Charney Vladeck, Benjamin Schlesinger, Chaim Zhitlowsky, Jacob Gordon, Sidney Hillman, Morris Winchefsky—just a few of the many idealists, self-seekers, business agents, and kindred brokers for the proletariat. We needed politicians, our own, to envision another world burgeoning from the dirt and the human excitements of the Lower East Side. We got them. . . .

Chapter 15
The Neighborhood Settlements

Though the year 1907 was one of minor economic panic—
Wall Street was riotous again—New York had its second greatest inundation of Jewish immigrants. They came, 148,000 possessed and dispossessed, past our street, Cherry Street, to attend
my circumcision, a *bris*; for I had been born just a week before.

They wandered by, my father told me years later, with their
elephantine bundles of baggage like so many peddlers looking
for a happy wedding, a simple customer, and a bed waiting for
an immigrant who unhappily brought with him lice. Our street
was part of the port, and Ellis Island was really our back yard
—out in the blue, windy harbor. The previous year had seen
even more Jewish immigrants—but not a panic. My brother
Mike had been born then, to join that year's 152,000 Jews from
Eastern Europe heading for thousands of stables, tenements,
rookeries, and cellars; to stay with fat uncles, slender cousins,
midget half cousins, forgotten friends, some real enemies—and
in temporary shelters created by various philanthropic societies,
especially The Hebrew Immigrant Aid Society—HIAS.

New York, with its laws making schooling for children manda-
tory, must have seemed quaintly democratic for the illiterate

HARRY ROSKOLENKO

East Europeans. Day schools, night schools, Sunday schools—
just off the greening buttocks of the Statue of Liberty—another
related neighbor, the city was an island demanding an American
education. An immigrant began with English and arithmetic. If
he had some Old World abilties, to run for office, he soon took
American history, civics, economics, law—any subject that
sounded American to an ambitious greenhorn preparing himself
on the unknown remnants of the old frontiers. How long ago
had he received the memorized letters about the fables of the
Goldeneh Medina—Manhattan's massively hidden gold mines? He
was now within the heart of the golden fables, the Lower East
Side, at night school or at a settlement school. For if you learned
nothing, you had to manage with ancient skills. Garbage collecting went to the classical Italians; becoming a cop or a fireman
to the clanning Irish; pants pressing, tailoring, the garment
trades, went to the ancient Jews—for the cultural processes of a
wandering history. At the Educational Alliance, where a Jewish
immigrant's real culture had its wider variations, a concerned
immigrant student made up his mind about how to mine the gold
metal lost between Fifth Avenue, Wall Street, and East Broadway.

Between 1900 and 1914, 1,435,000 forced-to-wander Jews
migrated to the United States, settling, in part, in streets around
the Lower East Side—Cherry, Monroe, Madison, Henry, East
Broadway, Montgomery, Clinton, Rutgers, Hester, Orchard,
Division—and farther north, north-by-east, east, swallowed into
the bolted-down city's many mysteries and miseries. But soon,
massively acquainted, the immigrant was off to a settlement
house, at night, for after-work American studies. During the day
he forcibly discovered the interior frontiers of the new industries and factories—and he was hardly a noble pioneer.

At the Educational Alliance, founded in 1893, I, not a greenhorn in 1913, went to study small nails, little hammers, short
saws—to become a junior carpenter. I would remake our Russian-Jewish home with American bookcases for my ten self-
owned books, found in a native garbage can; with a stool, to sit

210

much closer to the big Russian stove; a chinning bar, to make more muscle and frighten some Irish; a towel rack for my private towel—and little things that would mean big things to me, still wondering then whether I would ever become four feet high.

With an old ruler, I measured myself. I was 46 inches tall; too short or too tall for a boy of seven. Whom could I ask? We had no height experts in my family. My future stool by the Russian stove, for comfort, depended on the length of my legs. I measured my legs as well, then drew up a plan for the stool. I would sit about a foot from the floor . . . and I, still a sub-junior carpenter, made a round seat to fit my bottom and four small legs to groove into the seat. Within a week I had a glued-together stool, which my mother used on Fridays to drop twelve pennies into the twelve *pushkes* in the cabinet over the sink. When she was not giving *charity*, I was back on the stool, warming myself by the stove, eating apples and black bread—and reading about the French, Colonials, British, and Indians civilizing each other with muskets and tomahawks.

At the overly attended Alliance classes, I studied subjects that I did not get, at my age, at public school. I was in a major hurry, like the rest of the East Side's soon-to-be-middle-class proletarians. Carpenter, about-to-be-mariner, Boy Scout, I knew about birds, flowers, tides, rocks—and how to repair a broken head, with bandages. For the Educational Alliance taught a sullen or a happy boy to be less violently errant, more decently dutiful, and almost properly American—with our East Side local combinations. There was an art school, which created, later, so much of New York's latter-day Ashcan art, with such students over the years as Leonard Baskin, Peter Bloom, Adolph Gottlieb, Zero Mostel, Ben Shahn—and the sculptor Sir Jacob Epstein, who became an Englishman after he had been an East European and an American. It was an alliance of American hope plus universal scope. All a boy student had to do was go there, try not to beat up the then-tough teachers—and he was due to become a doctor in twenty years, so well trained that he would never be sued for malpractice.

If you were a sickly pale, underweight, bronchial boy and your mother was a talking *baleboosteh*, she quickly convinced one of the Alliance's many extraterritorial departments that her son, about to die from every known form of undernourishment, must have a two-week free vacation at Surprise Lake Camp—some miles from New York, in middling mountains, with natural cows, and a lake to swim in. I never managed to get there despite my mother's *baleboosteh* abilities. I was too husky, red-cheeked—and much too healthy. Selling newspapers had a mysterious vitamin attached to the news.

The few who managed to go to camp saw the green depths of natural things—and that was their shock. Other settlement houses ran summer camps for the earlier Irish and the later Italians, but we were not integrating in our holy ghettos and camps. We lived alone by elected choice, with our Yiddish speech and our complex differences. But we did integrate on the fire escapes—our tenement–summer camps. There we bedded down at night to get the salting breeze coming off the East River, to watch a fluttering pigeon splatter up the thick bedding, and to be soaked with summer rains. I liked the thunder of those days, for our camps resembled, by our normal differences, a two-story Judaic mountain suddenly flowering on Cherry Street.

There was a Mother's Department at the Alliance, hoping to teach young mothers to become older mothers, and another department for girls interweaving between the alerted mothers. There were sewing classes, homemaking studies, dance socials, and gymnasiums—but nothing about sex. It was a taboo subject despite the low bastard rate in those days. Today the pill and teen-age pregnancy are the Alliance's extracurricular concern.

There was music at the Alliance, with fiddlers, pianists, and quartets; and there were children's study halls, men's reading rooms, a religious education department, for Torah studies, as well as Yiddish, Hebrew, Russian—and accented Litvak. One day a boy running between his house and the Alliance's many cultural departments would cease to run, and become the man his father was not—a cultured American.

Philanthropy created the Educational Alliance and every

THE TIME THAT WAS THEN

other settlement house . . . and we used to say, as if rebuking the philanthropists, that money donated was conscience money. Such philanthropy was, however, the Judaic thing to do, according to my mother, who called it *tsdoke*—giving; a form of spiritually accented charity that did not rob the receiver of his dignity. And there we were, dignified, at the holier-than-us Alliance, blessed with things that were good to do, our egos normal, our pockets empty but learning to fill them up a bit as we discovered who our philanthropists were. Isidor Straus, of Straus's department store, was the president of the Alliance between 1891 and 1912. The others included Julia Richmond, Louis Marshall, Adolph Lewisohn, Felix M. Warburg, Jacob Schiff, Henry Morgenthau—*di raykher*, the rich—most of them German Jews. We were the sons of Russian and Polish Jews, trying to reach the cultural status of the *Yekes*—as we called the German Jews, rich or poor.

Actors about-to-become actors many years later, came to the drama department of the Alliance—like John Garfield, né Julie Garfinkel. Nat Holman, master basketball coach for City College, came to the basketball department to coach; later, thousands of champions before they acquired their hernias and charley horses. Future journalists came there to learn how to write: George Sokolsky and Eugene Lyons, as did future judges —George Z. Medalie and Jonah Goldstein—to acquire legal distillations on mayhem in New York City. There was another sculptor besides Epstein who had been taught at the Alliance, Jo Davidson—who molded all the ghetto's brashness . . . and since the Alliance gave courses in philosophy, there was the most unique teacher, Morris Raphael Cohen, who had learned some of his philosophical methods in Yiddish, Polish, and Russian at the Alliance's pragmatic school for genteel greenhorns.

Today it is a changed Alliance, for others live in the leftover slums and the public housing: Puerto Ricans, Chinese, Negroes —and some old Jews.

The new immigrants have changed the accents now that

213

years have come and gone. Where there were synagogues, today there are store churches or empty places. The Alliance, as an edifice for the scholar, is still very much as it was; the roof, where we played basketball, has been rebuilt for other, blacker, Nat Holmans. The brick-yellow exterior has been sandblasted, and new buildings, straight up, robbed of architecture, have been added for the newer problems of another time.

Dope addiction has taken the place of some learning for the young. The bastard rate is much higher. For the old, or those who have remained or come back to the ghetto, an apartment house, ten stories high, called the David L. Podell House, has been built for the aged—in time to celebrate the seventy-fifth birthday of the Alliance, the nation's second-oldest settlement house. It sits, squat, large-windowed, bulging over an old corner—and the spot where hundreds of thousands of immigrants and native-born pushed through its huge wooden doors at 176 East Broadway, across from Seward Park Library, a block from *The Forward*, and still the neighborhood's raw conscience. Ritualistic, historical, the playing place of the memory, the Alliance adopted boys who became corporate squires, like David Sarnoff—to ease them into an upward cultural thrust for those who could adapt. But there were the others who became gangsters, dying in a hurry. They too had been Boy Scouts, junior carpenters, amateur geologists, and mariners—but with Murder Incorporated.

I've returned often to the Educational Alliance—or the Hebrew Technical Institute as it was then dual-named—to walk around the blocks and see, yearly, how the new and the old can permanently bastardize an area. My last guide one January morning in 1970 was the souvenir book of a fair held in 1895 to celebrate the founding of the Alliance. It then sold for fifty cents. It has 144 shiny pages, and the cover, in reddish-brown, has symbolical figures—a girl with braided hair studying at a table; a young man, mustached, aproned, working at a lathe; and the three symbols of the Alliance wreathed together: an open book, an oil lamp with a wick, and a gavel, for order. Inside there are photos of the East Broadway of another day and

214

portraits of the founders of the Alliance. There are advertisements related to 1895s festooning graces as New York became a financial-industrial-commercial city. One ad, by the Mackay Cable Company, shows the final splice of the third Atlantic Cable—joined together a hundred miles out in the Atlantic . . . then the five portraits of the men who created the Alliance— Joseph Bloomingdale, vice-president; James Hoffman, vice-president; in the center, Isidor Straus, president; then Sam Schaeffer, vice-president, and Albert Hochstadter, secretary.

On page three of the souvenir book there is an ad for toys, leather goods, oil paintings, water colors, books, and things for gracious greenhouses—and it is Bloomingdale's ad. A Bradstreet financial ad on the next page states that their capital and surplus amounts to $1,500,000—and I wonder if my father knew about their cool surplus when he was a presser in a steaming loft on Greene Street.

There are ads for colorful scarves and suspenders. One for Borden's Milk, then produced by the New York Condensed Milk Company, shows a white horse, a white-dressed milkman, a bottle of white milk—and a little white wagon, with the legend "By it *we deliver absolutely pure, rich and wholesome milk*, the product of the very best dairies, produced under the most *scientific and hygienic principle—the result of 38 years' experience.*" Below are seven listings of depots serving Manhattan, Brooklyn, and New Jersey. I used to see the neat driver with the white horse and the white bottles, though he never stopped at 362 Cherry Street . . . and what milk I got I stole from Breakstone and Levine's liberal dairy, across the street from us.

Time gone, time here, time replacing itself into print, pictures, ads—a past world squeezed into our now plastic world. "The Imperial Hair Regenerator restores gray hair to its original color." In 1895, when my mother arrived, she was blond— unrestored. She wore corsets, soon enough. An ad on page 32 shows a lovely lady pulling on her corset stays; her waist, hourglass; her buttocks, full. On page 36 a Negro boy holds a white cat over a fence as he says in an ad selling printing and cata-

215

logues, "Say! is this your Cat-alogue Season?" What would my parents have made of that?

The official souvenir shows all the interior workings of the Alliance and the Institute; a machine shop, with men over turning lathes; pretty girls and handsome women with little caps, in a cooking class, making *gefilte fish* and *tsimmes*; an instructor and his young pupils, at mathematics; boys and men waiting or reading at the Aguilar Free Library; the immense Hebrew Orphan Asylum at 138th Street and Amsterdam Avenue. And how we worried when my mother would say *how lucky we were to have parents*. "When they built it during the Civil War it was not that far away in the country. . . ." and my father, an expert on orphans, like all immigrant Jews, interrupted, to add, "It was begun on Twenty-ninth Street and it only had thirty-three children then." Later there were thousands. Their parents had died in the *Goldeneh Medina*—and soon a boy had another home. It was a place that I dreaded. It meant no parents, no relatives—just blue jumpers; a barracks of imagined terror. But on the East Side we were all orphans in some strange way—with parents.

There were many other settlements, smaller, more harassed, five blocks east or ten blocks north of us. Near Brooklyn Bridge; off Manhattan Bridge, abutting Williamsburg Bridge—like the Henry Street Settlement. Begun by a nurse, Lillian D. Wald, in 1893, in a small house on Henry Street, it was soon as institutional as the august, yet spare, All Saints Church, built fifty years earlier just across from Nurse Wald's midwiving services for the East Side's future progeny. My mother had been visited, for birth pains and delivery, six times by the settlement's blue-dressed, buxom ladies. I was the fifth, and for the services rendered by the settlement my name should have been Henry, and one of my sisters Lillian. My mother, after the delivery, could only recall that she was in a Jewish panic about the nurse mixing up the dairy dishes and the meat dishes; that she sat up, watched the handsome nurse cooking in all of the intermingling pots, washing down the stove and the dishes like a master washer.

216

But all the dishes and pots that had been cooked in at random were also soaking together in the sink . . . and my mother had cried out, "Please, Mrs. Nurse, you have committed a sin—but it is my sin. That pot is *flayshedig. Oy, gotenu!* That other pot is *milchedig.* We'll have to make a *shila* when I get out of bed. Please, Mrs. Nurse, put that *milchediker* pot away!" My mother could scarcely contain her impatience to get up and cleanse the dishes.

The Henry Street Settlement was more than *milchedikes,* fresh-born babies, and nursing. It was to create a great theater on Grand Street—among its other aesthetic and social chores. The mixed-up pots were put away by all sorts of settlements; for the arts, coming up from tenements and sinks and cellars, were burgeoning over the ghettos.

Madison House at 300 Madison Street was founded by men who had ethics in their minds—the Downtown Ethical Society. The building was soon too small and they moved to 216 Madison Street in 1910, to provide quarters for more students reading the Talmud. It was not a real yeshiva. It went with baseball, wrestling, chess—but it did draw from the spiritual heritage to make some bearded rabbis, solemn Jewish philosophers, and Talmudic commentators. But if you continued walking down Madison Street, you soon reached the battlements of Manhattan Bridge, where the worst street fights took place between amateur scholars and professional brawlers. Heads, arms, legs, were broken. Under the bridge were warehouses storing great wine barrels; and when the wine and the blood mixed, it was a *goyishe yontev;* though the settlements, with their socially inspired morality, tried to change some of that in our muscles and hearts. It was *Christ-killing Jew bastard* and *Mick bastard,* which was not much of a choice. I alone had, roughly, killed Christ seventeen times when I went walking past the Madison House and found myself, about to be bloodied, under the Manhattan Bridge.

When I came back, bloodied, my father, who had no sympathy for my non-newspaper-selling wanderings, would ask, before I got the thunder of his orthodox dissent:

"Was it an Irisher?"

217

"No!" I was washing my bloody nose at the sink.

"Ah Poll-yack?"

"Maybe. . . ."

"What do you mean—maybe?"

"I did not have time to ask. They hit, I hit—and then I ran home."

"Did you hit well?"

"Yes."

"With blood, too?"

"With blood, too—and teeth."

"Teeth? Another boy's teeth? *A shande!*" And my father, opening my mouth, still full of teeth, slapped my face, shouting, "Never the teeth and never the eyes—*smarkatsh!*"

"And a hole in the head?" I asked, having given up crying at his rigid ways. "Is a hole in the head all right?"

"Not in your head! Read—don't walk under bridges!"

It took place fifty-five years ago in the inner spaces of half a century of other pilgrims' progressions. What I got besides nails, saws, hammers, lessons in dead reckoning, civics, the Torah, Yiddish poets, playwrights, lectures on *Eretz Yisroel*— was myself. I merged with a flood that had washed in earlier from Eastern Europe; a lonely kid less lonely, made into a student of all sorts of books. I read to read what I thought would mellow my early rebellions, but it did not, then. One night I rushed off to sea, and the world of the Educational Alliance and the Lower East Side dissolved in the crow's nest. Every image streaming up from Cherry Street was to blow past the Statue of Liberty, Emma Lazarus's *mezuzah*, once the tall signpost for every Jewish immigrant. 1 was reversing my father's route of 1895—when East Broadway, like Cherry Street, was the Jewish immigrant's permanent ghetto. I had other boundaries, none of them self-imposed, for the next seven years, when every port in Europe became part of my natural schooling. *The time that was then* was between my father's and mine.

NEW JERSEY

to Ellis Island & Statue of Liberty

Upper New Yo